# A World of Communities

**Text by**
Denise L. Babcock and Christine Lund Orciuch, Atlantic Group
Marcia S. Gresko

**Content Advisor**
John-Paul Bianchi
New York City Social Studies Consultant

**BLACKBIRCH PRESS**
*A part of Gale, Cengage Learning*

© 2009 Gale, Cengage Learning

**LIBRARY OF CONGRESS CATALOGING-IN-PUBLICATION DATA**

Babcock, Denise L.
  A world of communities student edition / Denise L. Babcock and Christine Lund Orciuch, Marcia S. Gresko.
       p. cm.
  Includes bibliographical references and index.
  ISBN 978-1-4103-0745-3 (hardcover)—ISBN 978-1-4103-0746-0 (pbk.)  1. Geography—Juvenile literature.  I. Orciuch, Christine Lund. II. Gresko, Marcia S. III. Title.

  G133.B22 2008
  910—dc22

                                          2008017891

Blackbirch Press
27500 Drake Rd.
Farmington Hills, MI 48331

ISBN-13: 978-1-4103-0745-3 (hardcover)   ISBN-13: 978-1-4103-0746-0 (pbk.)
ISBN-10: 1-4103-0745-X (hardcover)       ISBN-10: 1-4103-0746-8 (pbk.)

Printed in the United States of America
1 2 3 4 5 6 7 13 12 11 10 09

# Table of Contents

# Chapter 1

# Where We Live

Imagine what you would see flying in a plane around the world. There would be tall, rocky mountains and deep canyons. You would see long, winding rivers and huge sand deserts. Your plane would travel over great cities, small towns, and farms.

Most of the earth is covered with water. There is not much land for people to live and to grow food. Where people live affects how they live. It affects what food they eat and what clothes they wear. It affects the kind of house they build.

Wherever people live, they are part of a community. In some **rural** areas, people belong to the same **ethnic group**. They share the same religion. They speak the same language. In cities, or **urban** areas, many people live together. They may be from all over the world. They eat different foods. They speak different languages. They also celebrate different holidays.

Yet communities of people all over the world are alike in many ways. They tell stories and celebrate holidays. They follow religions and enjoy special foods. They build homes, raise families, and teach their children. They work, play, and make arts and crafts. Learning about communities around the world is important. It helps us understand how and why people are different from us. Learning about others is also a great way to understand who we are.

# How Geography Connects the World

**Geography** is the study of the world. It explores, people, places, and the land. There are five ideas that show how geography connects the world. The five ideas are **location**, **place**, **human-environment interaction**, **movement**, and **region**.

**Location** tells you where a place is. In this book, for example, you will learn about a "gentle" rain forest that is located in a small mountain area on the island of Puerto Rico.

*Mt. Everest is part of the Himalayas. It is located in Asia between Tibet and Nepal.*

4

**Place** tells you what a place is like. It tells you about the physical features. You can find mountains, rivers, beaches, plants, animals, and climate. It also tells you about the features that people make, such as roads, bridges, and cities.

In this book, you will explore many interesting places. In China, for example, you'll discover the Great Wall. The wall is thousands of miles long. It is also thousands of years old. The Great Wall protected the Chinese people from enemies. The wall kept out armies who rode horses.

**Human-environment interaction** tells you how people and the environment affect one another. It tells you how people use the land where they live. People use the environment in different ways. They build cities. They develop farmland. In dry areas, people build dams for water. In wet areas, they use boats to travel from place to place. In Chapter 7 of this book, you'll read about

*Big Ben is a famous landmark in London.*

*People in India built the city of Mumbai into a center of business and industry.*

the National Water Carrier system in Israel. Most of Israel is desert. The people of Israel built pipelines and canals to move water from the Sea of Galilee to cities and towns all over the country. The water helps farmers grow food and raise animals.

**Movement** tells you how people, goods, and ideas get from place to place. People bring ideas and things with them as they move to new places. In this book, you'll discover that settlers from England brought their

*This photograph shows two girls from different regions in China. Each one wears traditional clothing.*

*Goods and people travel by camel across a desert.*

language, sports, and other activities to countries such as South Africa and India. Many of these English traditions are very popular today.

**Region** tells you what makes one area like another area. A region can have the same plants. The people may speak the same language. They may have the same religion. In Russia, for example, some people that live in the eastern region of the country speak a language that is different from the people who live in other areas of the country.

6

**Continents and Oceans of the World**

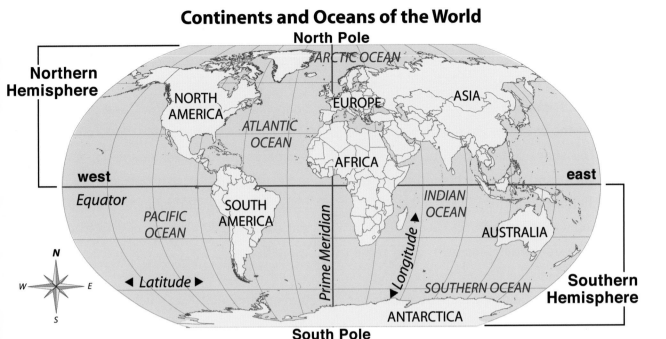

# The World of Maps and Globes

What is the highest point in China? Where are South Africa's gold mines located? What is the capital of Russia? Where do most people in India live? The answers to all these questions can be found on maps.

A map is a carefully drawn picture of the earth. It could also be just a part of the earth. Maps are important tools. They give us all kinds of information. Travelers use them to plan trips. Scientists use them to study the weather. Airplane pilots use them to find their way through fog and clouds.

You have probably used maps yourself. Have you ever looked at a directory in the mall? Have you ever seen a drawing of all the rooms in your school? Have you ever seen a drawing of where the exhibits are in a museum? If you have done any of these things, you have used a map.

There are many kinds of maps. There are maps of your city, your state, your country, and your planet. There are even maps of the moon and maps of the ocean floor. To find the capital of Russia you need a **political map**. It shows you capital cities, large cities, and the borders between countries. A **physical map** helps you find where rivers are. It shows important natural features—jungles, deserts, and mountains. Some maps have special information. They are called **special purpose maps**. They show different kinds of information. You can find information about climate, natural resources, or population density. You look at a **natural resources map** to locate South Africa's gold mines. If you looked at a **population density map**, you would see where most people live in India. A **climate map** tells you what the weather is like in England.

Maps can answer many questions. But you need to know how to read them. Some maps use names. Some use special colors and shapes. Lines and little pictures, **symbols**, all mean something special on a map.

There are four important direction words on a map. **Direction** means "which way." **North** is the direction toward the North Pole. It is shown at the top of the map. **South** is toward the South Pole. It is shown at the bottom of the map. **East** is the direction where the sun rises each morning. It's on the right side of the map. **West** is the direction where the sun sets each evening. It's on the left side of the map. Most maps have a **compass** that shows these four directions.

# What Do Globes Tell Us?

A globe is a model of the earth's surface. On the globe, there are imaginary lines. These lines tell people where different places are on the earth. You will see the word *equator* on most world maps. But even if you flew all the way around the world, you would never actually see it. The **equator** is an imaginary line around the wide middle part of the earth. It divides the earth into two equal parts. The **Northern Hemisphere** is above the equator. The **Southern Hemisphere** is below the equator. Many other imaginary lines appear on a map. **Lines of latitude** go around the world in the same direction as the equator (from left to right). You can tell how far north or south a place is by looking at them. Lines of **longitude** go around the

world from the North Pole to the South Pole (from top to bottom). They can tell you how far east or west a place is.

The **map legend** or **map key** helps you understand the colors, lines, and pictures you see on a map. For example, an airplane symbol might stand for an airport. The color green may show were forests are. On most maps, a circle or dot indicates a major city. A star usually shows the location of a country's capital.

One other thing you will see on the map. It is mostly blue! That's because more than 70% of the earth's surface is covered by water. The Atlantic Ocean, the Pacific Ocean, the Indian Ocean, the Arctic Ocean, and the Southern Ocean are earth's major

## Key Map Terms

**Equator:** imaginary line around the wide middle part of the world

**Longitude:** lines that go from top to bottom

**Latitude:** lines that go from left to right

**Northern Hemisphere:** area above the equator

**Southern Hemisphere:** area below the equator

**Star symbol:** capital city

**Circle or dot:** major city

bodies of water. These oceans separate huge land masses called **continents**. The seven continents are Asia, Africa, North America, South America, Antarctica, Europe, and Australia. Remember! Six of the continents all begin with the letter "A." All the continents end with the same letter they begin with!

## Geography Terms (See map on page 10.)

**bay:** Part of a lake or an ocean that extends into a shoreline.

**beach:** Strip of sand or pebbles where land meets water.

**canyon:** Deep and narrow valley with steep sides.

**cliff:** Steep, high wall of rock, ice, or earth.

**coast:** Land beside a sea or ocean.

**delta:** A rich area where a river deposits soil as its mouth.

**desert:** A dry area with little water where few plants grow.

**dune:** A hill of sand shaped by the wind.

**glacier:** A large area of slowly moving ice.

**gulf:** A large part of an ocean that extends into the land; larger than a bay.

**harbor:** Protected place along a shoreline deep enough for ships to dock.

**hill:** Raised area of land that is smaller than a mountain.

**horizon:** The line where the sky and the earth seem to meet.

**island:** Body of land surrounded by water.

**lake:** Body of water surrounded by land.

**mesa:** Hill or mountain with a flat top.

**mountain:** High landform with steep sides that rises more than 1,000 feet; higher than a hill.

**mouth (river):** Place where a river flows into a larger body of water.

**oasis:** Place in a desert where there is water from underground springs, and plants and trees grow.

**ocean:** Large body of salt water that surrounds the continents.

**peninsula:** Area of land that sticks out into the water, surrounded on three sides by water.

**plain:** Flat, rolling lowland, often covered with grasses.

**plateau:** Flat, high area of land higher than the surrounding land.

**rain forest:** Dense, tropical forest where a lot of rain falls.

**river:** Large stream of water that flows from a source into a lake or ocean.

**sea level:** Position on land level with the surface of a nearby ocean; a reference point for elevation—the highest or lowest points on the earth's surface.

**source (river):** Beginning of a river.

**steppe:** A flat, treeless plain often found on the edge of deserts.

**strait:** Narrow body of water connecting two larger bodies of water.

**valley:** Low land between mountains or hills.

**volcano:** A cone-shaped opening in the earth's surface where ash, melted rock, and gases escape.

**waterfall:** Water from a stream or river that falls from a high place to a lower place.

Geography Terms Map

Horizon · Volcano · Island · Mountain · Source (river) · Cliff · Peninsula · Glacier · Beach · Bay · Waterfall · Valley · Hill · River · Lake · Rain forest · Mouth (river) · Plain · Delta · Plateau · Mesa · Canyon · Desert · Harbor · Strait · Oasis · Dune · Coast · Steppe · Sea level · Gulf · Ocean

# Chapter 2
# England

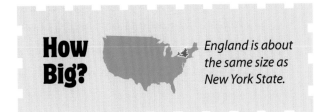

**How Big?** England is about the same size as New York State.

It is a long plane flight across the Atlantic Ocean to England. But when you land, you may feel that you have not left home at all! This is not so surprising. A little more than 200 years ago, the United States was an English **colony**. Our language and many of our laws come from English **traditions**.

Find England on the map. It is part of a European nation called The United Kingdom of Great Britain and Northern Ireland (UK). This nation is made up of four countries. They are England, Scotland,

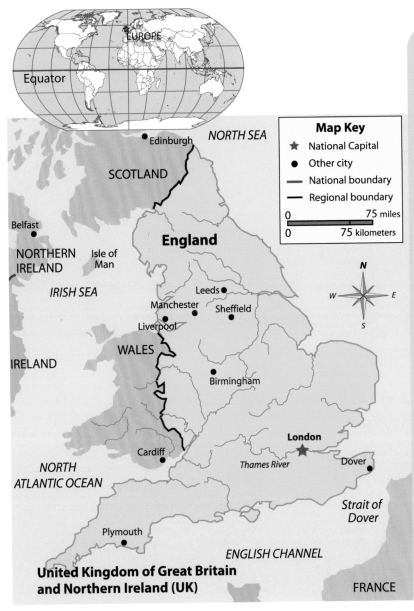

**Map Key**
★ National Capital
● Other city
— National boundary
— Regional boundary
0 — 75 miles
0 — 75 kilometers

## At a Glance

**Official name:** United Kingdom of Great Britain and Northern Ireland

**Capital:** London

**Area:** 50,352 square miles (130,410 sq km)

**Population:** 50,093,100 (UK: 59,834,300)

**Form of government:** Constitutional monarchy

**Chief crops:** sugar beets, potatoes, wheat, barley, dairy products

10% rural / 90% urban
**Population Distribution**

**Major industries:** food processing, iron and steel, electronics, textile production, cars

**Natural resources:** coal, petroleum, natural gas, sand, gravel, clay, limestone, salt

**Basic unit of money:** Pound. One pound is equal to about $2.05 US dollars.

**Main languages (U.K.):** English, Welsh (about 26% of the population of Wales), Scottish form of Gaelic (about 60,000 in Scotland)

**Major religions (U.K.):** Anglicanism (Church of England), Roman Catholicism, Islam, Presbyterianism, Methodism, Sikhism, Hinduism, Judaism

Wales, and a part of Ireland called Northern Ireland. England is the largest country in the UK. It is part of the island of Great Britain. England lies northwest of the **continent** of Europe.

England is north of the **equator**. That means it is in the **Northern Hemisphere**. Find the Irish Sea and the North Atlantic Ocean on the map. They are on the west coast. The North Sea is on the east coast. The English Channel separates England and France by about 21 miles. In 1994, the

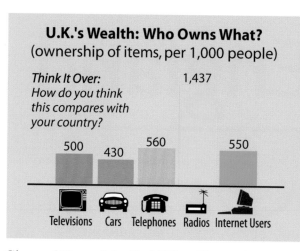

**U.K.'s Wealth: Who Owns What?**
(ownership of items, per 1,000 people)

*Think It Over:*
*How do you think*
*this compares with*
*your country?*

Channel Tunnel (called "The Chunnel") was built. It connects England and France. Most

# Activity

**1. Look at the map on page 11.** What four areas make up the United Kingdom?

a._____     b._____

c._____     d._____

**2.** Use the map. Imagine that you are in London. In which direction will you travel to get to Cardiff in Wales?

_____

**3.** England is located on a large island. Why do you think the county's location is good for trade?

_____

_____

**4.** Look at the bar graph. List two items that the people of the United Kingdom own the most of.

a._____     b._____

of the Chunnel is under water. Now trains carry passengers and freight between the two countries using the tunnel.

England is a small, crowded country. Its total land area is a little more than 50,000 square miles. It is about the size of the state of New York. A little more than 50 million people live in England.

In the north and southwestern areas are rugged highlands. In the center and southeast are low-lying **plains** and valleys. Most people live in these areas.

England's long coastline makes fishing an important **industry**.

England also has mild winters. This is because of the North Atlantic Current. It brings warm waters and winds from the Caribbean Sea to the British coast. Palm trees can grow in southwestern England. This current keeps England green all year long.

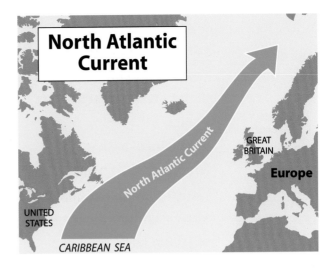

92%. This piece of the pie graph includes English, Scottish, Welsh, and Northern Irish. These peoples settled in the country over thousands of years.

The second largest group is Asian. Most come from Pakistan and India. The third group is Afro-Caribbean. They are mostly from the West Indies. England needed workers. These **immigrant** groups came to England looking for jobs. But many workers face **prejudice**. It is hard to find good jobs. It is also hard to find good places to live.

# The Many Communities of England

England's communities are an interesting mix of **tradition** and change.

## Ethnic Communities

There are three major **ethnic groups** in England. The largest group is **descended** from different European peoples. It is shown on the pie graph as White

**Ethnic Divisions of the United Kingdom**

Indian 2%
Black 2%
Pakistani 2%
Other 2%
White 92%

## Religious Communities

Most of the people in England are Christian. But the country has religious freedom. That means people are free to have different faiths. The Church of England is the official church of the country. It is also called the Anglican Church. The **monarch** (king or queen) is its head. It is a Protestant church. But services and religious practices vary. More than half

13

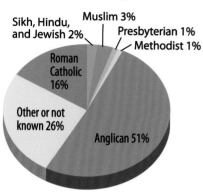

**Major Religions of the United Kingdom**

Sikh, Hindu, and Jewish 2%
Muslim 3%
Presbyterian 1%
Methodist 1%
Roman Catholic 16%
Other or not known 26%
Anglican 51%

of the English people belong to the Church of England. Roman Catholics make up the second largest religious group.

**Muslims** make up the largest group of non-Christian people in England. Muslims follow the religion of **Islam**. Islam teaches a belief in one god called Allah.

England has many people who practice other religions. Some of these religions are Sikhism, Buddhism, and Hinduism. The country also has one of the largest Jewish populations in Europe.

## Artistic and Cultural Communities

England is well known for its many famous writers. William Shakespeare wrote plays more than 400 years ago. They are still read and performed in countries around the world. Lewis Carroll, the author of *Alice in Wonderland*, was English. So was Beatrice Potter who wrote *The Tale of Peter Rabbit*. Charles Dickens wrote *A Christmas Carol*, the famous holiday story. J. K. Rowling, the author of the *Harry Potter* books, is also from England.

## At a Glance

### Holidays and Festivals

#### ★National Holidays

**Trooping the Colour:** Second Saturday in June. Celebrates the queen's official birthday. The queen inspects the troops that make up her personal guard. Cannons fire a salute and bands play.

**Armistice Day:** Sunday closest to November 11. Honors those who died in world wars. A procession is led by the queen. Wreaths are placed at a memorial.

#### ★Religious Holidays

**Christmas and Easter:** Celebrated as they would be by Christians in other countries.

**Maundy Thursday:** The day before Good Friday. The queen gives out specially minted coins to poor men and women.

### ★Other Holidays

**Guy Fawkes Night (Bonfire Night):** November 5. Remembers the plot by Guy Fawkes to blow up Parliament almost 400 years ago. Celebrated with bonfires, pranks, fireworks, and the burning of straw dummies or "guys." Similar to American Halloween.

**Boxing Day:** Day following Christmas Day is a public holiday. There are many different ideas about how this holiday began, but people spend the day with their families. People also give tips, or money, to service people—those who deliver milk or newspapers, door attendants, and so on.

**Chinese New Year:** Falls on the first day of the lunar calendar. Famous celebration in Chinatown, Soho. Paper lanterns decorate the sidewalks and a model of a dancing lion makes its way down the streets.

In the 1960s, rock-and-roll music was changed forever by an English group called the Beatles. They had many hit records. The Rolling Stones, Eric Clapton, and Elton John are other famous English superstars.

## Daily Life

Life in England is much like life in the United States. Most English people live in

## Word Watch

One of the most popular sports in England is football. But it is not football the way you think of it. In England, football is what Americans call soccer. What is like American football? It is the game called rugby.

## Activity

1. How do you think the North Atlantic Current affects people living in England? How do you think it affects the economy?

   a. _____

   b. _____

2. Look at the pie graph for **Ethnic Divisions**. White is the largest group with 92%. Which group do you think makes up the largest part of that group—English, Northern Irish, Scottish, or Welsh? Explain your answer.

   _____

   _____

   _____

3. Look at the two pie graphs. Why is it important that there is religious freedom in England? What might be the advantage of living in a country that has many different religious groups?

   _____

   _____

   _____

urban (city) places. Most people work in service jobs. These types of jobs include banking, health care, and transportation. Other service jobs are education, tourism, and retail stores. People also work in manufacturing jobs. In the countryside, there are modern cattle and sheep farms.

## Educational Communities

If you visited an English classroom, you would probably feel right at home. Like you, the children speak English. That is England's official language. But their English is not exactly the same as yours. If you spoke to some kids, you would find that certain words are different. They would say "ta" for "thank you." "Ring me up" means "call me on the phone."

All children between the ages of 5 and 16 must go to school. About 90% of children go to free state schools. The government pays for this. Boarding schools are common in England as well. Starting in the elementary

### Learn a Skill

The **main idea** of a paragraph tells what the paragraph is mostly about. As you read, look for the most important idea in each paragraph or each section. Then look for **details** in the paragraph or section that **support** the main idea.

grades, students live at school instead of at home. They visit with their parents during school holidays. Parents must pay to send their children to boarding schools.

## Communities of Friends

Outdoors, kids skate and ride bikes. People also like to go to parks. Indoors, board games are popular. Kids also like computer games. Snooker, a game like pool, is also fun.

*A teacher helps a student during a math class at Millfields Community School.*

16

*Football, which Americans call soccer, is the most popular sport in England.*

There are thousands of sports clubs across the country. Most English kids take part in at least one team sport. Soccer is the most popular.

Friends enjoy playing, going to watch their favorite teams compete, and trading soccer cards (like baseball cards). Cricket is like baseball. Players use a flat bat and a ball. It is very popular, too. It has been called England's national sport.

## Family Communities

Many English families own their own homes. Land is **scarce**. For that reason, homes are often smaller than homes in the United States. Many of the houses in towns are attached to one another. They look like row houses here in the United States. Gardening is a popular hobby in England. Most homes have a small garden. People grow flowers and vegetables.

Pets are important family members. About half of all English families have pets.

Sunday lunch is a family **tradition**. Eating out is a special treat. Fish and chips (french fries) is the favorite English "fast food."

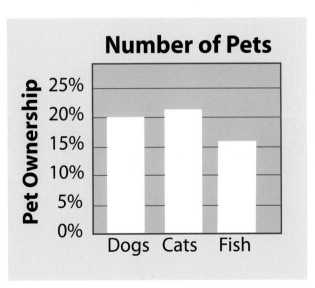

**Number of Pets**

17

# Activity

**1.** Pets are an important part of English and American life. Make a list of the pets that your classmates have. Add up the total number for each pet. Use that information to make your own bar graph below.

**Pet Ownership in My Class**

Title: _____

Number of Pets

Type of Pet _____    _____    _____    _____

**2. Apply Main Idea/Supporting Detail.** Read the following sentences. Circle the main idea sentence. Draw a line under the supporting detail sentence.

Pets are important family members. About half of all English families have pets.

**3.** Here are some everyday words used by kids in England. Can you figure out what they mean?

a. cooker _____     b. lift _____

c. bobby _____     d. sweet _____

e. bonnet and boot of a car _____

**4.** In this chapter of the book, you learned that England is an island. What might be a disadvantage of living on an island? Explain your answer.

_____

_____

# London

London is the capital of the United Kingdom. It is also the capital of England. London is one of the world's largest and greatest cities. About 7 million people live here. Millions of people from all over the world visit London each year.

London is a very old city. The earliest settlers in London lived along the River Thames. As time passed, they built villages. These people fished, farmed, and hunted.

Romans came to Britain in AD 43. The city of London was named by them. There are still reminders that the Romans once lived there. In fact, you can still see parts of the wall they built around the city.

London is a **port** city. Ships travel up the River Thames from the ocean. That has helped to make it a center for business. England depends on world trade. Banks, insurance companies, and shipping firms do business with countries around the world. The most important part of the economy is tourism.

Like many large cities, London has lost most of its manufacturing jobs. But London still has a small **manufacturing** base. This is because of the city's location on the river. There are clothing, metal works, and printing companies.

London's clock tower is named Big Ben. It is one of the city's most famous landmarks. The clock face is 23 feet across. Each number is 2 feet tall.

Important government buildings are located in London. The Houses of Parliament are there. This is where laws are made. So is Buckingham Palace. This is the official home of the royal family.

## Learn a Skill

**Graphs** and **charts** organize information into a picture. Look at the line graph on this page. It gives you a lot of information very quickly and clearly.

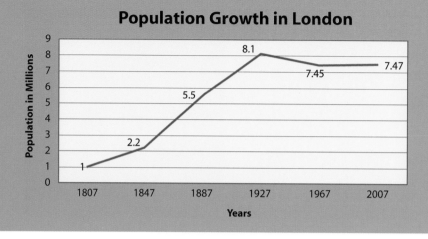

**Population Growth in London**

Westminster Abbey is the most famous of England's churches. Kings and queens have been crowned there for **centuries**. England's royal family no longer rules the nation. It is ruled by a prime minister, a group of government officials (called the Cabinet), and a Parliament (like a congress).

History is everywhere in London. St. Paul's Cathedral is almost 300 years old. It has become a **symbol** of London throughout the world. The well-known Tower of

*The Tower of London and Traitors' Gate taken from a boat on the Thames. Prisoners entered the tower by boat from Traitors' Gate.*

20

 **Activity**

**1.** Find London on the map of England on page 11. Why do you think London was built at this location on the island?

_____

_____

**2.** Why do you think the city became England's most important business center?

_____

**Apply Understanding Graphs.** Study the line graph on page 20. Then answer questions 3–5.

**3.** What is the subject of the graph? _____

**4.** In what year did London have the largest population? _____

**5.** Based on the growth graph, what would likely happen to London's population by 2047? Explain your answer.

_____

_____

London is a palace that was turned into a prison. It is the city's most historic landmark. It is nearly 1,000 years old.

## On the Tour Bus

Your plane has landed. You are in London. Now the fun begins.

London is exciting. There are theaters, museums, and parks. There is also a **multicultural** population. That means there are people from many different countries. You will learn about different religions and traditions.

A river trip is the best way to see London. Sail down the River Thames to Greenwich. Clocks all over the world are set by Greenwich Mean Time. You can stand at Greenwich Meridian. This imaginary line divides the world into the Eastern and Western Hemispheres.

*(Below) The lights of Festival Pier, the London Eye, Palace of Westminster, and the Hungerford Bridge at night. (Right) Standing on the prime Meridian of the world at Greenwich.*

Or you might climb the 521 stairs to the top of St. Paul's Cathedral. But if you really want a bird's-eye view of the city, go to the London Eye. This giant Ferris wheel is 443 feet high. The trip takes 30 minutes. From the top, you can see 36 Thames bridges, 7 countries, and 3 airports.

Don't forget to try some of England's famous foods. You might have Toad in the Hole. Don't worry. There are no toads. It is sausage cooked in a batter called Yorkshire Pudding. Have a great trip!

## Activity

Can you imagine living in London? What do you think might be different? What might be the same? Imagine you are moving to London. Make a list of questions you would want the answers to before you move there.

_____

_____

_____

_____

# Chapter 3
# Russia

Russia is the world's biggest country. It is almost twice the size of the United States. If you visit a certain place in Russia, you can stand on two different **continents** at the same time. About one quarter of Russia is located in Europe. The rest is located in Asia. Russia is north of the **equator**. That means it is in the **Northern Hemisphere**.

The Ural Mountains mark where Europe ends and Asia begins. They also divide Russia into two main areas. West of the mountains is European Russia. East of the mountains is Asian Russia. It is also called Siberia. Siberia has many important natural resources. However, much of the ground is always frozen. This makes it very hard to use Siberia's many resources.

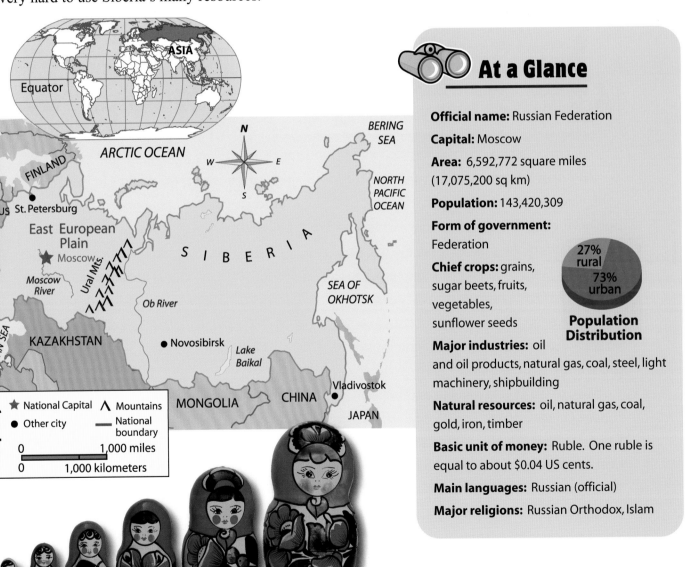

## At a Glance

**Official name:** Russian Federation

**Capital:** Moscow

**Area:** 6,592,772 square miles (17,075,200 sq km)

**Population:** 143,420,309

**Form of government:** Federation

**Chief crops:** grains, sugar beets, fruits, vegetables, sunflower seeds

**Major industries:** oil and oil products, natural gas, coal, steel, light machinery, shipbuilding

**Natural resources:** oil, natural gas, coal, gold, iron, timber

**Basic unit of money:** Ruble. One ruble is equal to about $0.04 US cents.

**Main languages:** Russian (official)

**Major religions:** Russian Orthodox, Islam

27% rural
73% urban
**Population Distribution**

23

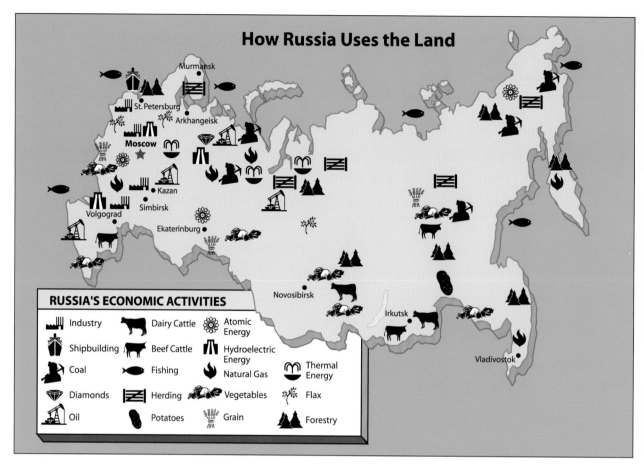

**How Russia Uses the Land**

RUSSIA'S ECONOMIC ACTIVITIES

|  | |  | |  | |
|---|---|---|---|---|---|
| | Industry | | Dairy Cattle | | Atomic Energy |
| | Shipbuilding | | Beef Cattle | | Hydroelectric Energy |
| | Coal | | Fishing | | Natural Gas |
| | Diamonds | | Herding | | Thermal Energy |
| | Oil | | Potatoes | | Vegetables |
| | | | Grain | | Flax |
| | | | | | Forestry |

Northern Siberia is mostly **tundra**. That is cold, bare, flat land. In the north, Siberia borders the Arctic Ocean. Freezing winters last eight months of the year. Few people live here. This is the home of polar bears and reindeers. The Pacific Ocean borders the east coast of Siberia. Eastern Siberia has mountains and active volcanoes. In the east, Siberia is only 50 miles away from Alaska.

West of the Ural Mountains is European Russia. On the map on page 23, find the East European Plain. This area is mostly a wide, flat, treeless **plain** called a **steppe**. Most Russians live in this area. It has rich black soil. The weather is milder. There is also plenty of rainfall. This area is good for farming.

Look at the land use map above. Find the forest symbols. Spreading across Russia's center from west to east is the world's largest **evergreen** forest. Cutting trees in the forest is a major **industry**.

Russia has many large bodies of water and rivers. Travel by boat is an important kind of **transportation**. Water also provides power to factories. The large fishing industry provides food for Russia's people.

**Russia's Wealth: Who Owns What?**
(ownership of items, per 1,000 people)

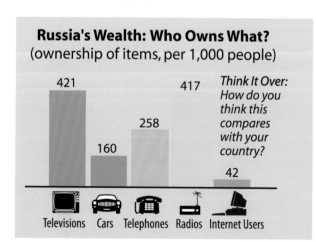

*Think It Over: How do you think this compares with your country?*

Televisions 421, Cars 160, Telephones 258, Radios 417, Internet Users 42

24

# The Many Communities of Russia

For a long time, Russia's different groups worked together to make a modern country. Today, Russia is changing. Its communities are changing too.

## Ethnic Communities

Russia has about 150 million people. They come from many places. About 82% of the people are of Russian **ancestry**. They came from a group of Eastern European people called Slavs. People in the Slavic group speak Russian.

**Ethnic Divisions of Russia**

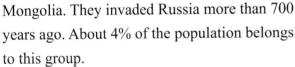

The second-largest **ethnic group** is the Tartars. These people came from Mongolia. They invaded Russia more than 700 years ago. About 4% of the population belongs to this group.

The third-largest group is the Ukrainians. They make up about 3% of the population.

About 100 other ethnic groups make up the remaining 11% of the population. These groups observe different religions and **traditions**. Their lifestyles have little in common. Many speak their own language. They use Russian as a second language. Because of these differences, some problems have occurred. Some ethnic groups want to break away from Russia. They want to form their own countries. These groups want to speak their own language. They want to practice their own traditions.

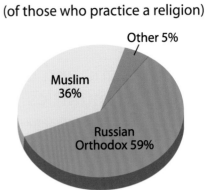

**Major Religions of Russia**
(of those who practice a religion)

## Religious Communities

For many years, Russians were pressured not to practice a religion. A person might lose their job for going to church. The government closed churches, mosques, and temples. Many were destroyed or used in other ways.

**Patriotic** holidays replaced religious holidays. Religious traditions for weddings, births, and deaths were not allowed. During this time, people practiced their religious faiths in secret. Today, people are free to enjoy their holidays and customs. The government does not outlaw religion.

The most common religion in Russia is Christianity. Most Christians belong to the Russian Orthodox Church. Their beliefs and practices are similar to those of the Catholic Church. The Russian Orthodox churches have beautiful onion-shaped domes. These domes fill cities and towns all across the country.

The second-largest religion in Russia is **Islam**. Followers of this religion are called **Muslims**. They believe in one God called Allah. Russia's Muslims live mostly in the areas that border central Asian countries.

The Jewish people have had a very hard history in Russia. They were often the victims of violence. When the Soviet Union broke apart, many Jews decided to leave the country. Many moved to Israel or to the United States.

## Artistic and Cultural Communities

Russia has a great **heritage** in painting, building design, music, and dance.

The country is well known for its music and ballet. Many famous composers were Russian.

Peter Tchaikovsky wrote famous ballets: *Swan Lake, The Nutcracker,* and *Sleeping Beauty*. They are still popular the world over. They are performed often by the two great Russian dance companies. These are the Kirov and the Bolshoi.

Russia's different regional ethnic groups also have rich cultural **traditions**. Communities have their own styles of lively folk dancing. The dancers wear traditional costumes.

# Activity

**Use the map on page 23 to answer questions 1 and 2.**

**1.** What is the capital of Russia? _____

**2.** You are in St. Petersburg. In which direction would you travel to get to the Caspian Sea?

_____

**3.** Do you live in a place that is usually warm or usually cold? How does your climate affect how you live?

_____

_____

**4.** Look at the land use map on page 24. Look at the area in the center of the map. Why are there no symbols in that area?

_____

**5.** Much of Siberia's ground is permanently frozen. Why does this make it difficult to use the country's many natural resources?

_____

# Daily Life

Russia was part of the Soviet Union for almost 75 years. That was an organization of 14 Communist republics. Under communism, the government controlled every part of daily life. Housing, clothing, food, and transportation were cheap. School and health care were free. People were given jobs for life. But the government also told people how to lead their lives. Russians did not have many freedoms.

In 1991, the Soviet Union broke up. Independent nations were created. During this change, many problems happened. Prices went up on all goods and food. People had trouble finding enough food, clothing, and housing. Many problems still occur.

Today, Russia is changing quickly. It has been trying to move toward democracy. That would mean the government is ruled by the people. But many people believe that democracy would not be good for the country. As Russia changes, there are many problems that need to be solved.

## At a Glance

### Holidays and Festivals

#### ★ Political Holidays

**International Woman's Day:** March 8. Honors women. Celebrated like Mother's Day in the US.

**Victory Day:** May 9. Most popular holiday. Marks the end of World War II. Celebrated with parades and fireworks.

**May Day:** May 1. Celebrates the arrival of Spring. Honors working people.

#### ★ Traditional Holidays

**Shrovetide (Butter Week):** Celebrated for 7 days at the beginning of Lent. Tricks, noisemaking, carnivals, and costumes are common festivities. A straw figure of winter is burned. People eat tasty filled pancakes called blini.

**New Year's Day:** Gifts are given and trees are decorated.

#### ★ Religious Holidays

**Christmas and Easter:** Celebrated as they would be by Christians in other countries. Easter is the most important holiday in the Russian Orthodox year.

*A Russian girl lighting a candle.*

27

## Activity

**1.** Imagine that you were not allowed to celebrate holidays. Which one would you miss the most? Explain why.

_____

_____

**2.** List three positive things the Communist government did for the Russian people.

a. _____

b. _____

c. _____

**3.** As you learned, the Soviet Union was made up of many ethnic groups. It was important to the Soviet government to create laws that

- told people what language they could speak
- did not allow certain holidays
- destroyed many churches and other religious buildings.

Why did the Soviet Union create these laws? How did these laws help the government? Explain your answers.

_____

_____

_____

_____

*Getting ready for class in elementary school.*

# Educational Communities

Education is very important in Russia. School is free for all students. Children must go to school from the age of 6 until the age of 17. Most parents work full time. So many children go to preschool. Here they learn to read and count.

Russian children go to school 5 or 6 days a week. Schoolwork is hard. Students with special talents in sports, music, dance, or math may go to special schools. Many students study two languages. More and more schools also have computers.

After ninth grade, students can go on to a regular school or to a trade school. Trade schools train students to work in farming or **industry**.

## Learn a Skill

A **pie graph**, also called a **circle graph**, is a tool that shows you how a whole can be divided into parts. The "pie" can be divided into "slices," or sections. To read a pie graph, read the title. Then read each label. Finally, compare all the pieces, or sections. The largest section shows you the largest part of the whole. The smallest section shows you the smallest part of the whole. If the graph uses numbers, they should add up to 100.

## Communities of Friends

Sports are a big part of most kids' lives. Soccer is the most popular sport in Russia. Kids also enjoy gymnastics, volleyball, and basketball.

Friends enjoy playing chess. It is Russia's national hobby. People also like to collect stamps. Stamp clubs are very popular.

## Family Communities

Almost three-quarters of Russian families live in crowded **urban** areas. Most rent small apartments in large housing projects. There are not enough apartments for everyone. Grandparents often share apartments with their children. Newly married couples may live with their parents for a few years.

Both parents usually work. Grandmothers often take care of the children. They shop for

*These two children live in northern Siberia. Here they welcome home a hunting party. The people hunt wild reindeer for food and clothing.*

the family. About two fifths of people work in factories. Another two fifths work in shops and offices. One fifth of Russians are farmers.

Shopping in Russia is hard work. Sometimes there is not enough food. Many times the food costs a lot of money. Clothing, shoes, and many household items may be hard to get. There are long lines in most stores.

Russian families enjoy their free time in many ways. People like to spend their vacations in the countryside. But only one in five Russian families owns a car. Families usually get there by public **transportation**.

# Moscow

Moscow has been the capital of Russia twice. The city was Russia's first capital. Then, for almost 200 years, the Russian city of St. Petersburg was the capital. About 80 years ago, Moscow became the country's capital city again.

Moscow is located in western Russia. The Moscow River flows through the city. The city is located far from the very center of the country. But it is at the center of Russian life.

One of Moscow's nicknames is the Hub City. Maps of the city show that Moscow is built in the shape of a wheel. In the middle is the Kremlin. It is an ancient walled fort. The Kremlin is now the center of the Russian government. The buildings inside its walls are a mix of old and new. There are grand palaces and beautiful churches. There are also important government buildings. Just outside the Kremlin is a large plaza called Red Square. Parades and other political events were often celebrated here.

All around the Kremlin area are many shops, modern offices, and cultural buildings. Moscow has a long history as the country's cultural center. There are almost 100 museums and art galleries.

*Cathedral of St. Basil at night. It is on Moscow's Red Square.*

There are also more than 1,000 libraries. A symphony orchestra and the famous Bolshoi Theater Ballet company are also located there.

Manufacturing districts surround the commercial and cultural areas. Moscow is Russia's most important city for **industry.**

Most people get around Moscow on the metro, or subway. The Moscow metro probably has the fanciest train stations in the world. Each station is decorated in a different style. They have glass lighting fixtures and large stone statues. They look like beautiful halls in a palace. Moscow is the **transportation** center of Russia. Highways and railways leave the city in all directions. They connect Moscow with the countryside.

Moscow has many of the problems that other big cities have. There is crime, pollution, and homelessness.

*Moscow metro (subway) at rush hour. Look at the columns and walls. They look like they belong in a palace.*

## Activity

1. **Apply Understand a Pie Graph.** Review the information about pie graphs on page 29. Then reread the second paragraph under **Family Communities** on page 30. Turn the information about how many people work at different jobs into a pie graph. Start by drawing a circle. You will need to divide the pie into 5 "slices." Color each section a different color. Be sure to label the sections.

2. Moscow is located on the Moscow River. How has the city's location helped it become a center for manufacturing and industry?

## Learn a Skill

Photographs can tell you a lot about how people live. To **analyze a photograph**, carefully look at the people or objects on the photo. Look at how the people are dressed. Study each item and the background of the photograph. Guess when you think the photograph was taken. Think about the conclusions you can draw from the information in the photo.

# From Vladivostok to Moscow

*Menia zovut Anya.* (min-ya-AH za-VOOT ahn-YA). That is Russian for "My name is Anya." Anya lives in Vladivostok. That is on the eastern side of Russia. Vladivostok is Russia's largest port. It is important for shipping, fishing, and as a home to a naval base.

Anya has cousins in Moscow. They have been waiting for her to come for a visit. Finally, school is out for the summer. Anya is on her way to Moscow. She is taking the Trans-Siberian Railroad. It runs from Vladivostok to Moscow. It is the longest single rail line in the world.

Moscow is 5,787 miles away. The train trip will take about eight days! Anya's father has bought her a ticket for a kupé. That is a small compartment. It has 4 beds in it. There is also a restaurant car. That is where Anya will have her meals.

On the way to Moscow, Anya wants to stop and see Lake Baikal. It is the deepest freshwater lake in the world. It holds one fifth of the world's fresh water. Anya talks to a tour guide that tells her about the pollution in the lake. Everyone is working to clean up the lake and to keep it clean. The trip will add on an extra day. But this Anya's vacation!

Finally, Anya arrives in Moscow. Her cousins are there to meet her at the station. So many people. So many things to do. First, she goes to Red Square. There she sees the onion-shaped domes of St. Basil's Cathedral. The domes are swirls of colors. To Anya, they look like huge balloons in the air.

People are everywhere. They walk slowly by the river. They wander through the parks. Anya walks by and looks at the posters for the Bolshoi Ballet. They will be performing *Swan Lake.* She would love to go, but it is expensive.

*View of the Moscow River and the Kremlin.*

33

Anya and her cousins take a break. They buy *pelmeni* (small meat pies) for lunch. They find the perfect place to enjoy lunch. The group sits next to a huge fountain. Fountains are a popular meeting place for friends.

It has been a long day. Anya is tired. They will all go back to the apartment. She looks forward to seeing her aunt and uncle. Tomorrow is another day. They will be off on a tour of the city. Anya will see a group perform folk dancing. Then it is off to the Moscow Circus. There are more than 7,000 performers! There is so much still to see. Anya is going to have a summer of fun.

## Activity

1. **Apply Analyzing a Photograph.** Your teacher will give you an organizer sheet for understanding photographs. Look at the photo on page 32, the Moscow Metro. Complete the organizer. What does the photo tell you about Moscow?

2. Why is it important that Russia built the Trans-Siberian Railroad? Explain your answer.

# Chapter 4

# China

**How Big?** China is a little smaller than the United States.

It is easy to find China on a map of the world. It takes up most of the eastern part of the **continent** of Asia. China is the fourth-largest country in the world. Only Russia (also located in Asia), Canada, and the United States are bigger.

On the map, find the national borders of China. Now find the 14 countries that border China. It shares its borders with more countries than most other countries in the world.

China is north of the **equator**. It is in the **Northern Hemisphere**. Most of China's east coast borders the Pacific Ocean. The coastline is about 9,000 miles long. The east coast of the United States is only 2,500 miles long. The US coast is only about one-third as long. China also has many islands. Two important islands are Hong Kong and Macao. The government claims that the island of Taiwan is a part of China.

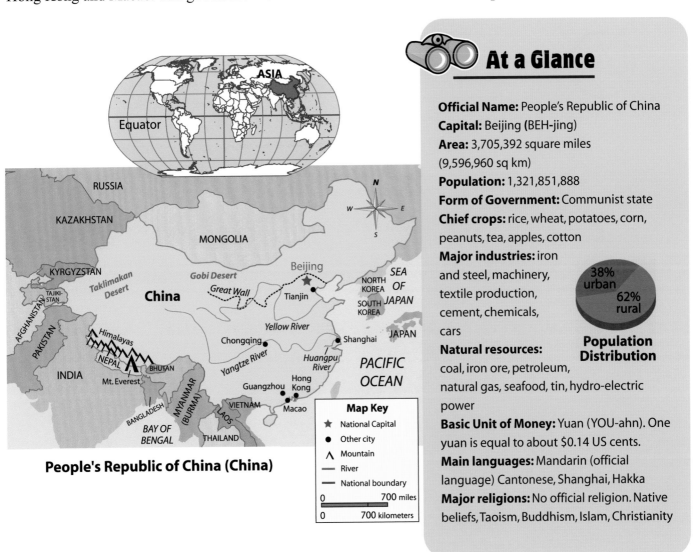

**People's Republic of China (China)**

## At a Glance

**Official Name:** People's Republic of China
**Capital:** Beijing (BEH-jing)
**Area:** 3,705,392 square miles (9,596,960 sq km)
**Population:** 1,321,851,888
**Form of Government:** Communist state
**Chief crops:** rice, wheat, potatoes, corn, peanuts, tea, apples, cotton
**Major industries:** iron and steel, machinery, textile production, cement, chemicals, cars
**Natural resources:** coal, iron ore, petroleum, natural gas, seafood, tin, hydro-electric power
**Basic Unit of Money:** Yuan (YOU-ahn). One yuan is equal to about $0.14 US cents.
**Main languages:** Mandarin (official language) Cantonese, Shanghai, Hakka
**Major religions:** No official religion. Native beliefs, Taoism, Buddhism, Islam, Christianity

38% urban
62% rural
**Population Distribution**

35

China has the world's largest population. More than 1.3 billion people live there. One out of every five people in the world lives in China. Most of the country is covered with deserts, mountains, and high **plateaus.** Only 15% of the land is good for farming. Many rivers in the east supply water. They also make **fertile** soil for farming. Most of the population lives in this area.

On the map on page 35, find the Himalayas in the southwest. It is the highest mountain range in the world. Mt. Everest is the highest mountain in the world. In the north, the Great Wall stretches 4,000 miles. This wall was built to keep out armies on horseback. It protected China from the West.

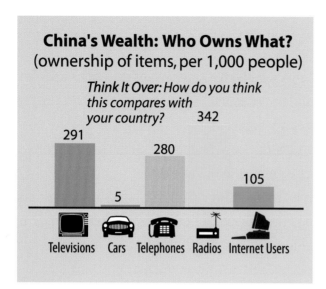

**China's Wealth: Who Owns What?**
(ownership of items, per 1,000 people)

*Think It Over: How do you think this compares with your country?*

Televisions 291, Cars 5, Telephones 280, Radios 342, Internet Users 105

# Activity

**1. Look at the map on page 35.** Name two bodies of water that border the east coast of China.

a. _____    b. _____

**2.** Use the map. Imagine that you are in Shanghai, China. In which direction will you travel to get to Japan?

_____

**3.** China has a large population. How do the landforms in China keep farmers from growing enough food to feed people?

_____

_____

**4.** Look at the bar graph, above. Explain what this bar graph is about.

_____

# The Many Communities of China

Most people in China are **descendants** of one **ethnic group**. This group is called the Han. The Han is the largest ethnic group in the world. Their **ancestors** lived along the Yellow River in northern China.

## Ethnic Communities

Many people speak different kinds of Chinese. Mandarin is the official language. Everyone learns to speak Mandarin. China's writing system is very old. It ties Chinese **culture** together. Chinese people can understand each other through writing.

About 8% of the Chinese people belong to different ethnic groups. They include Tibetans, Koreans, and Manchus. Each group has their own language and religion. They also have their own type of dress and way of life. Most ethnic Chinese live in communities far away from the cities.

China's population is huge. Millions of people live in crowded cities. About one third of the population lives in **urban** areas. In the cities, people burn coal for heat and to cook. This causes water and air pollution. The rest of the people live in **rural** areas. In the countryside, people work as farmers and laborers. They have few modern conveniences.

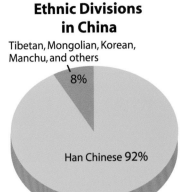

**Ethnic Divisions in China**

Tibetan, Mongolian, Korean, Manchu, and others 8%

Han Chinese 92%

*Two girls from different ethnic groups wear traditional clothing.*

## Religious Communities

The Chinese government controls religious belief. Officially, that is because China is a **Communist** country. Communists believe that religion stops progress. Many Chinese say that they are **atheists.** Atheists don't believe in any god. But many people still have religious beliefs.

Some people follow traditional Chinese religious practices. These beliefs include many gods and fortune-telling. The people also honor their **ancestors**. Other important ideas come from Confucianism, Taoism, and **Buddhism. Confucianism** is based on the teachings of an important Chinese leader. His name is Confucius. He taught that duty to family is important. He also taught people to obey the laws and rulers of the country.

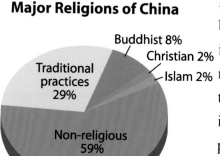

**Major Religions of China**

Buddhist 8%
Christian 2%
Islam 2%
Traditional practices 29%
Non-religious 59%

## At a Glance

### Holidays and Festivals

#### ★National Holidays

**May Day:** May 1. Also known as International Workers' Day. Honors working men and women around the world. Celebrated with family picnics, dancing, and fireworks.

**National Day:** October 1. Chinese independence day. Celebrates the formation of the People's Republic of China. There are speeches, parades, fireworks, and sporting events.

**New Year:** Also known as the Spring Festival. Celebrated for five days in January or February. Special foods, fireworks, parades, dragons, and lion dancers are all part of the festivities.

#### ★Other Festivals

**Qing Ming:** The "Clear and Bright Festival" comes in April. Families honor their dead relatives. They bring picnics to the cemetery and clean grave sites.

**Mid-Autumn Feast:** A harvest festival of thanksgiving. Families light colorful lanterns and enjoy traditional moon cakes. These cakes are filled with a sweet sticky paste.

*Lion dancers celebrate Chinese New Year in Beijing.*

**Buddhism** came to China from India. It arrived in China about 2,000 years ago. Buddha taught that the soul is reborn many times on its way to becoming perfect. **Taoism** is based on the ideas of the teacher Lao Zi. It encourages people to live in harmony with nature.

## Artistic and Cultural Communities

China has a long history in the arts. Their beautiful paintings have been done for thousands of years. The subjects come from nature. They include mountains, water, trees, birds, and flowers. A painting usually includes

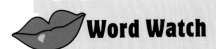 **Word Watch**

One of the most popular ways to celebrate the New Year is with fireworks. The Chinese invented fireworks over 2,000 years ago. They filled a bamboo tube with gunpowder and tied it to a stick. They called these early fireworks "fire arrows."

a poem. The poem is written in black ink with a brush. The brush writing is called **calligraphy**.

 **Activity**

1. Reread the section on **Ethnic Communities** on page 37. What two ways of communication help tie Chinese culture together?

   a. _____     b. _____

2. Look at the pie graph for Chinese ethnic groups. What might be the benefit of living in a country with one major ethnic group? Why is it important to protect the rights and freedoms of minority groups?

   _____

   _____

3. China has the largest population in the world. But only 15% of its land is suitable for farming. How does this small amount of farmland make life difficult for people in China?

   _____

   _____

39

*Performers in the Beijing Opera wear colorful makeup and costumes.*

The Chinese learned to make silk. They boiled silkworm cocoons. Then people spun the fine threads into silk. The silk trade helped spread Chinese culture throughout Asia. Artists also made a new kind of pottery called **porcelain**. The thin, white porcelain became very popular in Europe. Chinese traders grew very rich.

People love to go to the Beijing Opera. Operas are stories told in song. They are very popular. Actors speak and sing in high singsong voices. The actors wear colorful makeup and fancy costumes. The colors stand for different personality traits. For example, a red face means bravery. A black face means strength. The "bad guy" usually has a white face.

## Educational Communities

China educates a huge population. Chinese children go to school six days a week. They start school at the age of 6 or 7. Students must attend school for nine years. They study many of the same subjects that you do, including English. Students also learn to read and write the difficult Chinese language.

All Chinese students learn to be good **citizens.** Special classes teach **patriotism.** That is a love of country. Children learn to be polite, honest, and responsible. But not every moment is spent in a classroom. Physical exercise and team sports are also an important part of every school day.

Most children in China go to school until they are 13. Students in **rural** areas have a

*Chinese students show their work in a fourth grade classroom.*

40

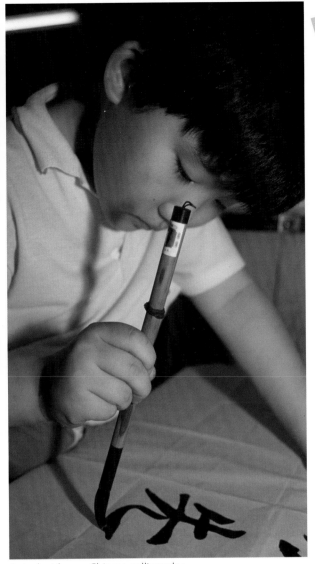

*A student learns Chinese calligraphy.*

## Learn a Skill

Often, an author asks you to **draw a conclusion** from what you read. You draw a conclusion based on the facts in what you read. Make sure the facts support your conclusion.

is no shortage of children. Chinese children love to play sports. They like soccer, basketball, and ping-pong. Kites were **invented** in China. Flying kites is a popular hobby. There is even a kite-flying festival in April.

## Family Communities

Family life is very important in China. Children are thought to be very special. Older people in the family are treated with great respect. Most young people live with their families until they get married. They usually marry in their late 20s or early 30s. Divorce is not common in China.

harder time going to school. They often must leave school to work in the fields or in factories. They need to earn money to help their families. Few children in China go to college. Colleges are very expensive. The entrance tests are also hard. China does not have enough teachers or schools.

## Communities of Friends

The Chinese government made laws to control China's huge population. Chinese couples in **urban** areas can have only one child. But there

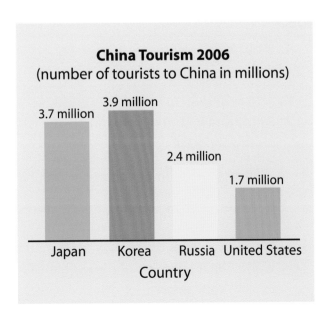

**China Tourism 2006**
(number of tourists to China in millions)

Japan 3.7 million · Korea 3.9 million · Russia 2.4 million · United States 1.7 million

Country

*Friends enjoy tasty food at an outdoor market.*

Chinese families enjoy doing things together. Meals are always special occasions. Tasty Chinese cooking is known around the world. Families also enjoy shopping in outdoor markets.

Chinese families and visitors from other countries enjoy sightseeing. Popular places include the Great Wall and the Forbidden City in Beijing. The Forbidden City was the home of Chinese emperors in the Ming and Ching dynasties.

 **Activity**

1. What is being compared in the bar graph on page 41?

_____

2. **Apply Draw Conclusions.** Circle the letter of the sentence that is the best conclusion for the bar graph.

   a. The largest number of tourists to China come from the United States.

   b. Most of the tourists to China come from Asia.

3. In this chapter of the book, you learned that China has the largest population in the world. What are some of the problems for people living in such a crowded country? Explain your answer.

_____

_____

# Shanghai

Shanghai is located at the mouth of the Yangtze River. The city grew from small fishing villages. Shanghai is the largest city in China. It is also the largest **port** in the world. The city is the center of Chinese trade and business.

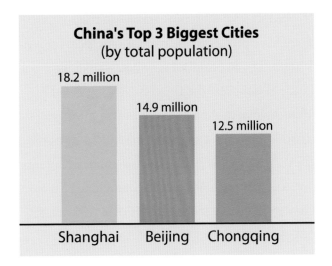

**China's Top 3 Biggest Cities**
(by total population)

18.2 million — Shanghai
14.9 million — Beijing
12.5 million — Chongqing

Over 18 million people live in Shanghai. Most people live in tiny apartments. So they spend a lot of time in outdoor activities. City parks are popular places to play and exercise.

Shanghai is a mixture of old and modern **cultures**. Like many cities in China, it is very crowded. People come from **rural** areas to

work in factories and businesses. Many ride bicycles to work. Homes and factories burn coal for fuel. This causes terrible air pollution.

A famous area in Shanghai is called the Bund. This road is a mile long. It stretches along the Huangpu River. On the west side of the road, there are grand old buildings. They were once owned by foreign banks. People called the Bund the "Wall Street of Asia." On the east side, there are tall modern buildings. Here stands the Pearl TV Tower and the Jing Mao Tower.

*Shanghai's modern tower is named the Oriental Pearl Tower. It is the tallest tower in Asia. The tower includes many shops and restaurants.*

People visit museums and eat in restaurants. They have picnics in the parks along the river. Visitors stay in beautiful new hotels, like the Peace Hotel. Near the Bund is Nanjing Road. Tourists love to shop here. Plaza 66 on Nanjing Road is the newest shopping mall. It features the latest fashions and American fast-food restaurants.

Another popular place in Shanghai is Yu Garden. This magical garden is over 400 years old. A son built the garden for his old father. Ancient stone walls surround the gardens. Carved dragons sit on top of the walls. Thousands of visitors cross the red wooden bridges. They stop to look down into lovely pools. Bamboo trees are made to look like tiny forests.

The Chinese love to watch and play soccer. Shanghai stadium holds over 80,000 people. People like to be outdoors. Many mornings you will see people in parks practicing tai-chi. This is an ancient form of exercise. In China, there are many American restaurants. They sell hamburgers, ice cream, chicken, pizza, and coffee. People eat traditional Chinese food at small noodle shops. People also drink a lot of tea. People use taxis, buses, a subway system, and bicycles to go to work.

## Learn a Skill

A **time line** shows events in the order in which they happened. This type of graph helps you understand and remember when events happened. A time line also shows how much time passes between events. The title tells you the subject of the time line. The dates at the beginning and end of the time line tell the period of time that is covered.

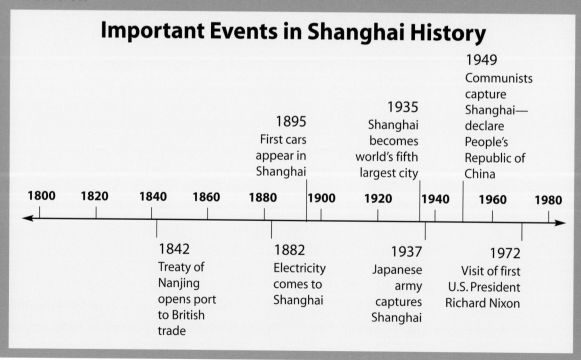

### Important Events in Shanghai History

**1949** Communists capture Shanghai—declare People's Republic of China

**1935** Shanghai becomes world's fifth largest city

**1895** First cars appear in Shanghai

1800  1820  1840  1860  1880  1900  1920  1940  1960  1980

**1842** Treaty of Nanjing opens port to British trade

**1882** Electricity comes to Shanghai

**1937** Japanese army captures Shanghai

**1972** Visit of first U.S. President Richard Nixon

## Activity

1. Look at the details in the photograph of Shanghai on page 43. List 3 ways that the river helps people who live in the city.

   a. _____  b. _____

   c. _____

**Apply Understand Time Lines.** Study the time line on page 44. Then answer questions 2–4.

2. What is this time line about? _____

3. Read the first and last date on the time line. What is the amount of time shown on the time line? Show your work.

4. In what year did Shanghai become the world's fifth largest city? _____

5. Name the first American president to visit China. _____

# Along the Bund

It is early morning in Shanghai. Mist drifts up from the Huangpu River. In the parks, older people move silently as they practice tai-chi movements.

You ride your bicycle along an old neighborhood street. You are far from the fancy shops of Nanjing Road. The weather is sunny and warm. Everyone seems to be outside. You wave to a barber. He shaves a customer. A woman cuts up onions and cabbage for her family's lunch.

Young children take baths in small tin pans. A man sits at a table on the sidewalk. He writes a letter for a customer. A lady wheels her cart of eggs through the crowds. She sells a special fast food. People like these 1000-year-old eggs! Over a steel-drum stove, a butcher cooks a duck.

In Shanghai, the smells of cooking and the sounds of street noise make the city an exciting mix of old and new China.

*The Great Wall winds across a hilly area near Beijing.*

## Activity

Imagine that your family just arrived in Shanghai. You came from the countryside. What type of work might you find? Where will you live? Do you need transportation? Make a list of the things you need to live and work in Shanghai.

_____

_____

_____

_____

## How Big?

India is a little more than 1/3 the size of the United States.

...m the United States. You cross the Atlantic Ocean, then fly over ...lly, you reach the huge continent of Asia. China and Russia are in ...of Asia. It is a part of Asia. But it is a separate landmass. The ...India from the rest of Asia.

...**orthern Hemisphere**. Look at the map. Southern India is ...est coast lies the Arabian Sea. On the east coast is the Bay of

...lation. More than one ...re people.

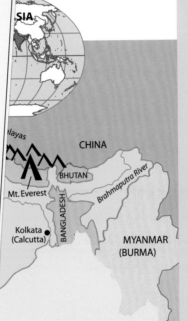

CHINA
BHUTAN
Brahmaputra River
Mt. Everest
Kolkata (Calcutta)
BANGLADESH
MYANMAR (BURMA)
BAY OF BENGAL
INDIAN OCEAN

### At a Glance

**Official name:** Republic of India

**Capital:** New Delhi

**Area:** 1,269,340 square miles (3,287,575 sq km)

**Highest Point:** Kanchenjunga, Himalayas, 28,208 feet (8,598 m) above sea level

**Population:** 1,129,866,154

**Form of government:** Federal Republic

**Chief crops:** rice, wheat, oilseed, cotton, jute, tea, sugarcane, potatoes

**Major industries:** textiles, chemicals, food processing, steel, transportation equipment, cement, mining, petroleum, machinery, software

**Natural resources:** coal, iron ore, manganese, mica, bauxite, natural gas, diamonds, petroleum, limestone

27% urban
73% rural

**Population Distribution**

**Basic unit of money:** Rupee. One rupee is equal to about $0.025, about 2½ US cents.

**Main languages:** Hindi (official) and English; 14 other official languages; 24 languages that are spoken by a million people or more

**Major religions:** Hinduism, Islam, Christianity, Sikh, Buddhism, Jainism

*Tourists visit the famous Taj Mahal in Agra.*

47

Some of the world's highest mountains are in northern India. They are part of a mountain range called the Himalayas. Below the Himalayas are high **plateaus**. The Ganges River flows through this region. The area has rich, fertile soil. There is plenty of water. Most of the population lives in this area.

*Hindus pray along the banks of the Ganges River in Varanasi, India.*

Find Pakistan on the map. Along the border with India, the weather is dry. Hot, dry winds blow over sand dunes. This is the Thar Desert. The desert has no water. No crops can grow here.

India has more than 4,350 miles of coastline (land beside an ocean or sea). Fishing and trade are two important **industries** (businesses). Most business and industrial centers are located on the coasts. Mumbai is the capital of business and industry in India. This west coast city has a deep **port**. This makes it easy for trade and fishing ships to dock here.

**Tsunamis** are giant ocean waves. They are caused by earthquakes. A tsunami can wash away a town in just a few minutes. They are a problem for villages along the east coast of India. The 2004 Indian Ocean tsunami killed thousands of people in eleven countries. Some waves were over 100 feet tall.

### India's Wealth: Who Owns What?
(ownership of items, per 1,000 people)

*Think It Over: How do you think this compares with your country?*

Televisions 75, Cars 6, Telephones 45, Radios 120, Internet Users 17

**Map of 2004 Indian Ocean Tsunami**

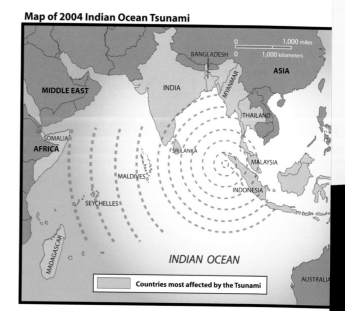

# The Many Communities of India

The people in India are a mix of **ethnic groups**. They have different religions, cultures, and traditions. Because Great Britain ruled India from 1857 until 1947, India also has some traditions from England. Let's look at some of the different kinds of communities in India.

## Ethnic Communities

There are three major ethnic groups in India. The largest group is called Indo-Aryan. They are about three-quarters of the population. People in this group have a mixed **ancestry**. They are a mix of native Indian and white European races. Indo-Aryans speak mostly English and Hindi.

The second-largest group is Dravidian. They make up a quarter of the population. They are a native Indian race. Common Dravidian languages are Tamil and Telugu. The third group is called Mongoloid. These people came mostly from China and Russia. About 3% of the population belongs to this group.

**Ethnic Divisions of India**

Mongoloid 3%

Dravidian 25%

Indo-Aryan 72%

## Religious Communities

Most of the people in India are **Hindu**. Hindus worship many different gods and goddesses. The three most important gods are Vishnu, Shiva, and Brahma. Every Hindu home has a **shrine** to the gods. Shrines have colorful flowers, beads, and small statues. People burn incense to please the gods. The Ganges is a **sacred** river to every Hindu.

Hindu families have a special ceremony. It is called the Thread Ceremony. This marks a son's change from boyhood to manhood. During the ceremony, a young boy and his father stand by a sacred fire. A sacred thread is placed on the boy's right shoulder and tied across his body. The boy will wear

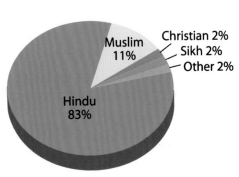

**Major Religions of India**

Muslim 11%

Christian 2%
Sikh 2%
Other 2%

Hindu 83%

the thread every day for the rest of his life.

The second-biggest religion in India is **Islam**. **Muslims** are followers of Islam. They make up about 11% of the population. Muslims believe in one God named Allah. They learn from a holy book called the Koran. Islam was founded by Muhammad. Muhammad is believed to be Allah's **prophet**, or messenger.

Two other religions are also important in India's culture. They are Jainism and Sikhism (SEEK-izm). Jains believe in nonviolence. Sikhs believe in the equality of all human beings.

## Activity

**Look at the map on page 47 to answer questions 1–2.**

**1.** What body of water is found along the east coast of India? _____

**2.** Use the compass rose on the map. What country borders India in the northwest?

_____

**3.** Look at the map of the 2004 tsunami in the Indian Ocean on page 48. Explain why it is a problem when houses are built too close to the coast.

_____

**4.** Study the bar graph about India's wealth on page 48. What one item do people of India own the **least** of?

_____ Why do you think that is so? _____

_____

## Artistic and Cultural Communities

Religion is part of Indian art. There are many famous religious landmarks. Statues of gods and beautiful temples are carved into the walls of cliffs. Graceful Indian dancers use their hands, feet, and fingers to tell stories. The stories are based on popular Indian myths and legends.

Traditional musicians play on stringed instruments, drums, gongs, and flutes. Puppet plays are very popular. The puppets are characters from wonderful folktales of gods and goddesses.

*Puppet plays are popular in India.*

50

Rudyard Kipling was a British author. He wrote a famous story called *The Jungle Book*.

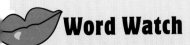

## Word Watch

Did you know that the word *pajamas* comes from India? *Pa jama* means "loose trousers" in Hindi. When the British governed India, they noticed many people wearing this style of pants. They decided the pants would be comfortable for sleeping!

The story takes place in Kanha National Park. Kanha is one of India's largest national parks. It is the home of leopards, deer, and the famous Bengal tigers.

## Daily Life

Daily life depends on where people live. About 73% of Indians live in **rural** areas. These areas have small farming villages. The rest of the population lives in cities and towns. India has a wet climate. Spring and summer are hot and wet. There is heavy rainfall. Rice is an important food in India. Rice plants need a lot of water to grow. India's climate is perfect for growing rice.

## At a Glance

### Holidays and Festivals

★**National Holidays**

**Independence Day:** August 15. Celebration of India's Independence from Britain in 1947.

**Republic Day:** January 26. Marks the anniversary of the beginning of the Indian Republic in 1950. Elaborate parades feature highly decorated elephants and camels.

★**Religious Holidays**

**Ramadan:** A month-long period of prayer and fasting for Muslims.

**Holi:** Hindu festival held in February or March. Celebrates the coming of spring. People run through the streets splashing each other with colored water and powder.

★**Other Holidays**

**Diwali:** Hindu New Year celebration that comes at the end of October or beginning of November. Known as the "Festival of Lights."

*Hindu women paint designs called mehandi on their hands and feet. They celebrate Diwali and other special occasions.*

In the past, India sorted people into four classes. The four classes were priests, rulers, farmers, and workers. This created a **caste system.** It divided people into groups based on their job and wealth. Poor people suffered under this system.

## Educational Communities

Only about one in three of India's adults can read and write. Education is free for children ages 6 to 14. Children are expected to go to school, but not everyone does. Most of India's children only go to school until the fifth grade.

## Communities of Friends

Many children in India have responsibilities. Farm children help with chores. They also take care of the family's animals. In the cities, children may help in shops or with younger family members. But everyone enjoys being

# Activity

**1.** Why is the climate so important for growing rice in India?

_____

_____

_____

**2.** Choose a festival or holiday from India. How is the festival or holiday similar to one that you celebrate?

_____

_____

_____

**3.** Write two or three sentences that explain how the Hindu Thread Ceremony might bring the culture of India together.

_____

_____

_____

(Left) School children in Makum, India, learn to read and write Hindi and Assamese. (Bottom) The game of cricket is played on a "pitch," or field.

with friends. Children play traditional games such as chess. It began in India. Girls like to play a game called Five Stones. It is similar to jacks. And all over India, children go to the movies. Even small villages usually have a movie screen and projector.

A favorite sport in India is cricket. The British brought cricket from England. It is played with a ball and a flat bat. There are only two bases. Imagine a team getting 200 runs in a game that can last for days!

## Family Communities

Family ties are very important in India. There is even a festival that celebrates the relationship between brothers and sisters. Sisters tie a decorated silk thread around their brothers'

wrist. Then they place a red powder dot on their own forehead. Sisters also prepare sweet foods for their brothers to show their affection. Brothers give their sisters several gifts and promise to defend them.

## Learn a Skill

A **cause** is the reason something happened. The **effect** is what happens as a result. First, identify an event. Find the cause or causes by asking, Why did this happen? Find the effect or effects by asking, What happened as a result? Signal words such as *because, since,* or *as a result* show cause and effect.

# Mumbai (Bombay)

In 1996, India changed the name of Bombay to Mumbai. Mumbai is an exciting city. It is also the capital of business and industry. More people want to live and work in Mumbai than any other city in India.

Many cities in India have difficult problems. People are poor. They live in **poverty.** The cities are overcrowded. In Mumbai, more than half of the population

**India's Top 3 Biggest Cities**
(by total population)

|  |  |
|------|-----------|
| Mumbai | 19 million |
| New Delhi | 14.1 million |
| Kolkata (Calcutta) | 14 million |

lives in **slums.** These people have no running water or electricity. Many people share one room in a building. Families might have to share one toilet with a hundred people.

But not all of Mumbai is poor. Because there is so much **industry** and business, Mumbai is also very wealthy. There are rich families. They have huge homes in the city's **suburbs**. They have air-conditioning, fancy cars, microwaves, computers, and many servants.

*Mumbai is the center of business and industry.*

# Activity

1. **Apply Cause and Effect.** Underline the cause and circle the effect in each statement.

   a. Because there is so much industry and business, Mumbai is a wealthy city.

   b. Rice grows very well in India, because there is heavy rainfall in spring and summer.

2. What three cities are shown on the India's Top 3 Biggest Cities bar graph.

   a. _____

   b. _____

   c. _____

3. You learned that Great Britain ruled India until 1947. List one way that British rule affected Indian culture.

   _____

# Learn a Skill

**Tables**, or **charts**, organize facts so they are easy to understand. Look at the table below. It shows you the amount of wheat, rice, and corn produced by 4 countries in one year.

## Production of Wheat, Rice and Corn, 2004
(in thousands of tons)

| Country | Wheat | Rice | Corn |
|---|---|---|---|
| China | 91,290 | 176,553 | 123,175 |
| India | 71,814 | 116,580 | 10,570 |
| Russia | 50,557 | 483 | 1,541 |
| United States | 43,992 | 9,568 | 228,805 |

Source: UN Food and Agriculture Organization

(Top) Bollywood movie posters in Mumbai. (Right) Crowds shop in a bazaar, or market, in Mumbai.

Mumbai is the movie capital of the world. One of its largest businesses is making movies. Mumbai is called "Bollywood." It produces more movies than Hollywood, California. Almost every Indian loves movies. If you walked along a crowded, noisy street in Mumbai, you would probably see someone making a movie.

## Daily Life in Mumbai

Mumbai has many different areas. There are beaches near the water. In the center of town, there are high-rise office buildings. Outside the city, families live in many different kinds of neighborhood communities.

# Visit a Neighborhood

Let's visit Tarang. He lives with his family outside the city. Tarang gets up early at about 5:00 a.m. He sleeps outside when the weather is hot. This helps him keep cool. He helps his family with chores. By 7:00 a.m., he walks to school with his little brother.

At school, Tarang studies Hindi, English, science, geography, history, math, and art. During recess, he plays cricket or soccer with his friends. School ends at 2:00 p.m.

Tarang eats a big lunch when he gets home. His mother packs a lunch for his father. Tarang takes it to his father's shop. His father owns a small shop. He sells snack food and cold drinks. The shop is close to a bus stop, so he gets a lot of customers.

While Tarang takes care of the shop, his father takes a break. At 5:00 p.m., Tarang goes home to start his homework. When his homework is done, Tarang plays outside until dark. Then he comes inside to watch TV. His family eats dinner together around 9:00 p.m. Tarang's favorite food is curry. It is hot and spicy. At ten o'clock, it is time for bed. Tarang will be up early again in the morning!

# Activity

1. **Apply Understand a Chart.** Study the chart on page 55. Then answer the questions.

   a. What is the title of this chart? _____

   b. What country grew the most rice in 2004? _____

   c. What country grew the most corn? _____

   d. Why does China produce so much wheat and rice? _____

   _____

2. Find Mumbai on the map on page 47. Then look at the photograph of Mumbai on page 54. Write one reason why Mumbai is a good city for business.

   _____

3. Your teacher will give you a T-Chart. Label one column in the T-Chart **Same** and the other column **Different**. Think about your daily activities and Tarang's activities. Then complete the chart to show how the activities are the same and different.

# Chapter 6
# Turkey

It is 7:00 a.m. in New York City. You are up and ready for school. In Turkey, it is 7 hours later. It is 2 p.m. Everyone has finished lunch. Students are ending their day. Turkey is a part of Southwest Asia. It is also part of the Eastern Mediterranean. This is the area of the world where three **continents** meet. These are Asia, Europe, and Africa.

Turkey is north of the **equator**. That means it is in the **Northern Hemisphere**. To Turkey's north is the Black Sea. To the south is the Mediterranean Sea. In the middle of Turkey is a large **plateau** area. Mountains rim the area. To the east, you will find the Tigris and Euphrates Rivers.

Look at the map of Turkey's climate on page 59. The center of Turkey has hot, dry summers. The winters are cold and snowy. Along the Mediterranean, summers are hot and dry. Winters are mild and rainy. Look at the area of Turkey by the Black Sea. It has heavy rainfall. The area has small fishing villages.

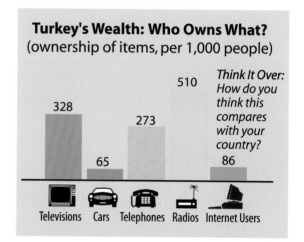

**Turkey's Wealth: Who Owns What?**
(ownership of items, per 1,000 people)

*Think It Over: How do you think this compares with your country?*

| Televisions | Cars | Telephones | Radios | Internet Users |
|---|---|---|---|---|
| 328 | 65 | 273 | 510 | 86 |

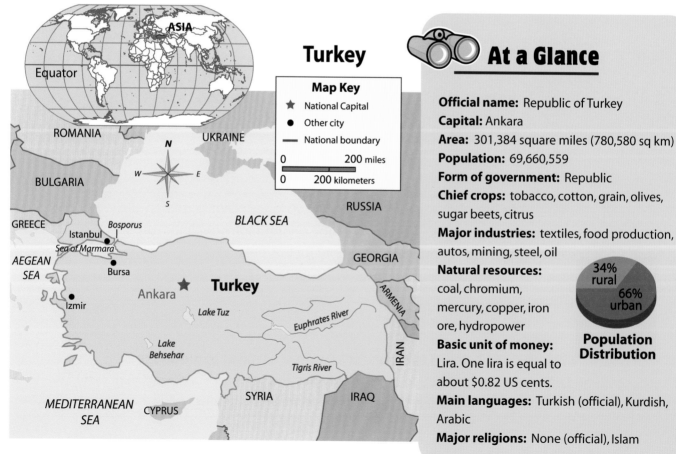

**Turkey**

**Map Key**
★ National Capital
● Other city
— National boundary

0 — 200 miles
0 — 200 kilometers

ROMANIA, UKRAINE, BULGARIA, RUSSIA, GREECE, Bosporus, Istanbul, Sea of Marmara, AEGEAN SEA, Bursa, Izmir, Ankara, **Turkey**, Lake Tuz, Lake Behsehar, BLACK SEA, GEORGIA, ARMENIA, Euphrates River, Tigris River, IRAN, MEDITERRANEAN SEA, CYPRUS, SYRIA, IRAQ

## At a Glance

**Official name:** Republic of Turkey
**Capital:** Ankara
**Area:** 301,384 square miles (780,580 sq km)
**Population:** 69,660,559
**Form of government:** Republic
**Chief crops:** tobacco, cotton, grain, olives, sugar beets, citrus
**Major industries:** textiles, food production, autos, mining, steel, oil
**Natural resources:** coal, chromium, mercury, copper, iron ore, hydropower
**Basic unit of money:** Lira. One lira is equal to about $0.82 US cents.
**Main languages:** Turkish (official), Kurdish, Arabic
**Major religions:** None (official), Islam

34% rural
66% urban
**Population Distribution**

58

## Turkey: Vegetation and Climate Maps

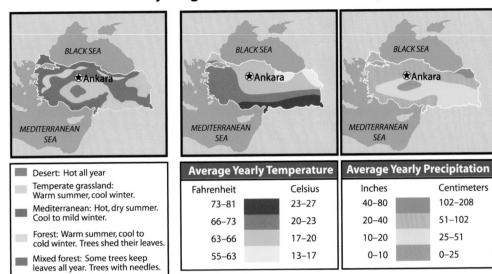

Desert: Hot all year

Temperate grassland: Warm summer, cool winter.

Mediterranean: Hot, dry summer. Cool to mild winter.

Forest: Warm summer, cool to cold winter. Trees shed their leaves.

Mixed forest: Some trees keep leaves all year. Trees with needles.

| Average Yearly Temperature | |
|---|---|
| Fahrenheit | Celsius |
| 73–81 | 23–27 |
| 66–73 | 20–23 |
| 63–66 | 17–20 |
| 55–63 | 13–17 |

| Average Yearly Precipitation | |
|---|---|
| Inches | Centimeters |
| 40–80 | 102–208 |
| 20–40 | 51–102 |
| 10–20 | 25–51 |
| 0–10 | 0–25 |

# Activity

**Use the map of Turkey on page 58 to answer questions 1–2.**

1. What body of water is to the north of Turkey? What body of water is to the south?

   a. North: _____     b. South: _____

2. Imagine that you are in Izmir. In which direction will you travel to get to Istanbul?

   _____

**Use the Vegetation and Climate Maps above to answer questions 3–4.**

3. How does the amount of yearly precipitation (rain and snow) affect the type of vegetation that grows?

   _____

4. How much rainfall does Ankara get in a year?

   a. _____

   What is the average yearly temperature in Ankara?

   b. _____

59

Turkey has a long history. About 8,000 years ago, it was home to some of the first farming villages. It has been controlled by Romans and nomadic people from Central Asia.

In 1453, the Ottoman Turks controlled the area. It was a very powerful empire. In World War I, the Ottomans fought on the losing side of the war. They lost all the land.

The war hero Mustafa Kemal (1881 to 1938) took over the government. He changed his name to Kemal Atatürk. That means Father of Turks. After World War I, he created a new Turkey. Before Atatürk, Islamic law shaped Turkish life.

Atatürk wanted a modern Turkey. He separated all religion from the government. He wanted people to wear Western clothes.

He encouraged women to stop wearing the traditional veil. He also wanted women to vote. Women could run for political office. Atatürk believed Turkey needed to be modern to become a strong nation. Today, many Islamic political parties want **Islam** to have more of a role in the government.

# The Many Communities of Turkey

Most of Turkey's 69 million people are ethnic Turks. Their ancestors came to Turkey from central Asia during the A.D. 900s. About 20% of the people are Kurds.

There is plenty of land in Turkey. But most of the people want to live in the same places!

About half of all the people live on less than one quarter of the land.

## Ethnic Communities

There are two **ethnic groups** in Turkey. The largest group is mostly **descended** from people from central Asia. Look at the pie graph. They make up 80% of the people.

The second largest group is the Kurds. They live in the mountainous area in the southeast. Many also live in the west. They make up 20% of the people.

**Ethnic Divisions of Turkey**

Kurdish 20%

Turkish 80%

## Religious Communities

There is no official state religion in Turkey. People have the freedom to choose their own religion. But almost everyone living in Turkey is **Muslim**. That means they follow Islam. It teaches the belief in one God called Allah. Islam was founded by Muhammad. He is called Allah's **prophet**, or messenger. The Koran is their holy book. People study the words from the Koran. It is part of how they live their daily lives.

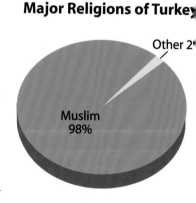

**Major Religions of Turkey**

Other 2%

Muslim 98%

Turkey also has a long history of Christianity. Turkey is where the followers of Jesus Christ were first called "Christians."

## Artistic and Cultural Communities

Turkey has a long history of creating beautiful arts and crafts. Turkey also has some of the most beautiful buildings in the world. The country is also known for its wonderful carpets. These hand-woven rugs have bright colors. Marco Polo was a famous Italian traveler during the thirteenth century. He wrote about these beautiful rugs.

Turks make wonderful bowls and tiles. Tourists come from all over the world to buy rugs, bowls, and paintings.

Early Turkish books were about poetry, oral history, and religion. Rumi is one of the best-known poets in the world.

 ## At a Glance

### Holidays and Festivals

★**National Holidays**

**New Year's Day:** January 1. Celebrated very much as it is in the rest of Europe and other Western countries.

**National Sovereignty and Children's Day:** April 23. All over the country, schoolchildren dress up in national costumes. They perform plays. The main celebration is in Ankara, the capital. Children from all over the world are invited to sing and dance.

**Atatürk and Youth and Sports Day:** May 19. Celebrates the Father of Turkey. Dedicated also to the youth of Turkey.

**Victory Day:** August 30. Dedicated to the armed forces. Celebrates the victory of Turkish Independence War of 1922.

**Mevlana Festival:** Held in December. Birthday of Mevlana Celaleddin-i Rumi. He was a famous poet and philosopher. He believed in and taught forgiveness.

★**Religious Holidays**

**Ramadan Feast:** A month long period of prayer and fasting observed by Muslims.

*Whirling dervishes at the Mevlana Festival twirl for hours to become closer to Allah.*

## Activity

**1.** List two ways that Kemal Atatürk made Turkey a more modern country.

a. _____  b. _____

**2.** Atatürk once said, "Peace at home is peace in the country. Peace in the country is peace in the world." What do you think he meant by this?

_____

_____

**3.** Do you think a religion should run a country and control the government? Explain why or why not.

_____

_____

_____

*A schoolroom in a Kurdish village on the border of Turkey and Iraq. War and unrest are making life very hard for people who live on the border.*

## Word Watch

Did you know that English has borrowed many words from Turkish? The word *tulip* comes from the Turkish word *tülben,* which means "turban" (a type of Turkish hat). A tulip looks like a turban. We have also borrowed the words *yogurt, bridge* (the card game), and *kebab* (meat on a skewer, or stick).

## Daily Life

Atatürk made many changes in the way Turks lived. Today, we can still see those changes. Most of the people live in **urban** areas and are middle class. About one third of the people live in **rural** areas in villages. There is a big difference in how they live. Middle-class Turks live very much like middle-class people in Europe. Most Turks who live in villages are more **traditional**. **Islam** is very important to how they live their lives.

Many people work in Turkish factories. The major **industries** are textiles, cars, paper products, and food production. But almost half of the people work on farms. They grow the food that feeds the Turkish people. They also grow extra food to sell to other countries.

## Educational Communities

Schools are free in Turkey. Turks believe that education is very important. They are working to improve their education. Today, the class sizes in many schools are smaller. Teachers have added computers and foreign language studies to their classes.

All children between the ages of 7 and 15 must go to school. Kurdish schools often struggle. At one time, people were not allowed to speak the Kurdish language in public. The government has tried to turn the Kurds away from their culture. This has caused many problems between Turks and Kurds.

After the age of 15, students can go to college. Some students go to training schools. Others go out into the job world.

## Communities of Friends

Turks love sports. Soccer is very popular. Some soccer fans paint their faces with the team colors. Other sports are also popular. You can find archery (bow and arrows), swimming, sailing, and wrestling. One very old sport is *jirit.*

*Players on horseback in a jirit game. It is similar to polo, except riders toss javelins at each other.*

63

## Learn a Skill

A **fact** is a statement that is true. "Millions of people live in Turkey." You can prove this. Look in an almanac or on the Internet. An **opinion** is what someone feels, thinks, or believes. "Turkey has the most beautiful buildings in the world." You cannot prove this. An opinion is neither true nor false. Ask whether the statement can be proved or disproved. If the answer is yes, the statement is a fact. If the answer is no, the statement is an opinion. Sometimes, opinions use words like *better, most, believe, always, happy, sad, best, worst, seems, should, love,* or *beautiful*.

It is like polo. But riders on horseback throw javelins (spears) at each other!

## Family Communities

To Western people, many customs in Turkey may seem old-fashioned. In some areas, parents still choose a husband or wife for their children. This happens mostly in smaller villages. Children usually live with their parents until they are married.

In rural areas, Turkey has a high birthrate. Families often have 7 to 10 children. Families in the city do not have as many children. Turkish families also take care of older people. They do not go to nursing homes. Older people go to live with their children.

What are the favorite foods in Turkey? Lamb, tea, and rice are popular. Pieces of lamb, tomato, onions, and peppers are grilled on a skewer. This is called shish kabob. Bread, yogurt, and eggplant are daily meals.

## Activity

Imagine that you are writing a chapter about life in the United States. Interview a classmate about his or her favorite food and favorite sport. Write a short paragraph that describes that person's favorite food and the sport. Try to include one fact and one opinion in the paragraph.

# Istanbul

Istanbul began as a Greek port called Byzantium. Later, the Roman emperor Constantine the Great renamed it Constantinople. That was more than 2,500 years ago. In 1453, Constantinople was renamed Istanbul. It was the capital. In 1923, Atatürk moved the capital of the newly formed Turkey to Ankara. Istanbul's location has made it a successful city. It is Turkey's largest city.

All through history, **geography** has had a say in where cities are located. You learned that London is on the Thames River. Moscow sits next to the Moscow River. Shanghai was built at the mouth of the Yangtze River. Rivers make it possible for cities to trade with other areas.

*Istanbul is the only city in the world that is located in two continents. The Bosporus strait separates the city. It also divides Europe from Asia. Here you can see the Blue Mosque (in front) and the Hagia Sophia.*

65

## Learn a Skill

Skim through the graphs that appear throughout this book. **Graphs** organize information into a picture. They give you a lot of information very quickly. It is also very easy to see that information clearly. You will make a graph in the Activity on page 67.

Istanbul's geography is similar to these other cities. Istanbul is the only city in the world that sits on two **continents**. Part of the city is in Asia. The other half is in Europe.

Look at the map on page 58. Find Istanbul. Notice that the Bosporus (BAHS-puhr-uhs) divides the city. It also divides Europe from Asia. The Bosporus is an important seaway. It connects the Black Sea in the north with the Sea of Marmara. That sea leads into the Mediterranean Sea. You can see that Istanbul's history is important to trade and **industry**.

Istanbul mixes modern buildings with old and beautiful landmarks. Find the Blue Mosque in the photograph on page 65. It is in the front of the photo. It is unusual because it has six minarets (min-uh-RETZ). A minaret is a tall, thin prayer tower. Most mosques have only four minarets.

Istanbul is like many other big cities. There is some crime. There is also **poverty**. Istanbul struggles with pollution and other big city problems.

## Discover Istanbul

You have finally arrived in Istanbul. Rest up. You will do a lot of walking and sightseeing. It takes time to see all of Istanbul. The city has been around for over 2,000 years. Istanbul is

*The Grand Bazaar is the oldest and largest covered marketplace in the world. It has 22 separate entrances. More than 25,000 people work here.*

filled with beautiful buildings, art, history, and great food.

You begin your day with a visit to the Grand Bazaar. It is the oldest and largest covered market in the world. It was started in 1455. In the sixteenth century, it was made even larger. It has more than 58 streets. There are over 4,000 shops. It is like walking through a maze.

But to shop at the bazaar, you need to know how. Tourists do not just pull out their wallets and pay for items. First, you must barter with the shopkeepers. This means you pretend you are not interested in what you want to buy. Then you say you can buy it somewhere else for less. Finally, you decide on a price you will pay. This is called haggling over the price.

Next stop is the Spice Market. The smells of fresh spices and cooking are wonderful. The market is noisy and crowded. You buy some grilled fish for lunch.

After lunch and a cup of Turkish tea, you are off again. The Blue Mosque was built in

# Activity

1. Look again at the map on page 58. Find Istanbul. Explain why the Bosporus is such a major shipping route.

_____

_____

2. **Apply Understanding Graphs.** Make your own bar graph below. In the graph, you will compare the population of three of Turkey's biggest cities. Be sure to include labels and a title. Here is the information you will use for your graph: Istanbul 10,291,102; Ankara 4,319,167; Izmir 3,500,000.

3. Using the graph you made, write two questions that can be answered by your graph. Then have a classmate answer the questions.

Question 1: _____

Question 2: _____

67

*For fresh fish and vegetables, visit the many markets in the streets of Istanbul.*

1609. It is famous for its beautiful tile. The Hagia Sophia, now a museum, was built by a Roman emperor in 537. It is breathtaking.

Before you go inside any mosque, you must know the rules. You have to take off your shoes. (In fact, if you visit a Turkish family, you will probably have to take off your shoes. Dirty shoes never go into clean rooms!) Do not wear shorts. Women should cover their heads, shoulders, arms, and legs.

Tomorrow you are off to visit two continents in one day! You will take a boat trip along the Bosporus. Along the shores, you will see ancient palaces and modern buildings. Be sure to take your camera.

*Iyi geceler.* "Good night."

## Activity

1. What is unusual about Turkey's largest city?

_____

_____

2. Carefully study the photo on page 66 of the Grand Bazaar. Read the caption. Write a description of how shopping in the bazaar might compare with shopping at a mall in the United States.

_____

_____

_____

# Chapter 7
# Israel

**How Big?** Israel is about the size of New Jersey.

When it is night in the United States, children in Israel are waking up for school. Israel is almost on the other side of the world. You fly east from the United States to reach Israel. Your plane crosses the Atlantic Ocean, Europe, and the Mediterranean Sea.

When you land in Israel, you are on a part of the Asian **continent** called the Middle East. Look at the map. Israel is a thin strip of land on the Mediterranean sea.

Israel is north of the **equator.** It is in the **Northern Hemisphere.** Look at the map key. Notice the areas in orange. The orange areas are in dispute. That means Israel and its neighbors disagree over who owns this land. Egypt, Jordan, Syria, and Lebanon fought wars with Israel over who owns this land. They still do not agree.

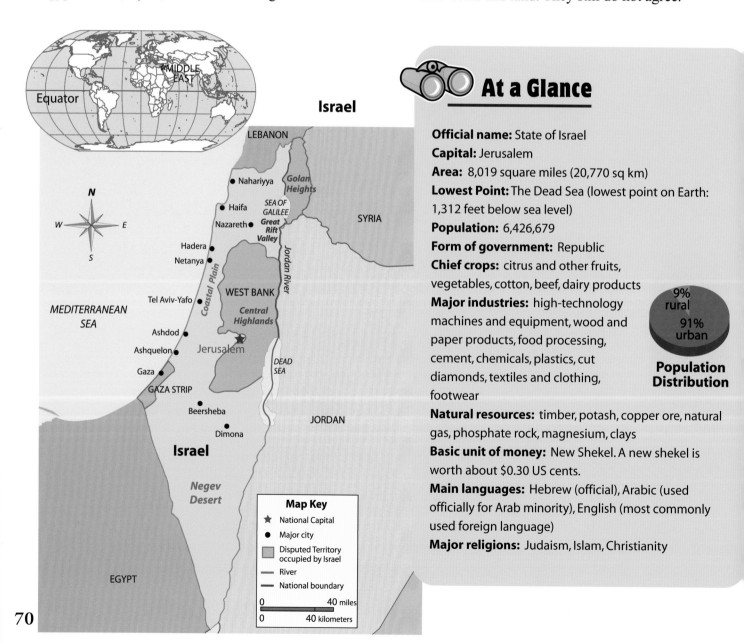

## At a Glance

**Official name:** State of Israel
**Capital:** Jerusalem
**Area:** 8,019 square miles (20,770 sq km)
**Lowest Point:** The Dead Sea (lowest point on Earth: 1,312 feet below sea level)
**Population:** 6,426,679
**Form of government:** Republic
**Chief crops:** citrus and other fruits, vegetables, cotton, beef, dairy products
**Major industries:** high-technology machines and equipment, wood and paper products, food processing, cement, chemicals, plastics, cut diamonds, textiles and clothing, footwear
**Natural resources:** timber, potash, copper ore, natural gas, phosphate rock, magnesium, clays
**Basic unit of money:** New Shekel. A new shekel is worth about $0.30 US cents.
**Main languages:** Hebrew (official), Arabic (used officially for Arab minority), English (most commonly used foreign language)
**Major religions:** Judaism, Islam, Christianity

9% rural
91% urban
**Population Distribution**

**Map Key**
★ National Capital
● Major city
▨ Disputed Territory occupied by Israel
— River
— National boundary
0 — 40 miles
0 — 40 kilometers

70

Israel is a tiny country. It is a little bigger than the state of New Jersey. Almost 6 and a half million people live in Israel. That is less than the population of New York City.

Israel may be small, but it has many landforms. The Mediterranean Sea borders the west coast. This region is a coastal **plain.** The temperature is warm. The area has **fertile** soil. There is enough water from rivers. Farmers grow **citrus** fruits. Fruit is an important crop for farmers.

**Industries** are also located on the west coast. They make **chemicals,** clothing, electronics, and cut diamonds. The Mediterranean Sea helps trade and **transportation** of goods. This area has a warm **climate.** The land is fertile. There are many job opportunities. All these make this region the most densely (heavily) populated part of the country.

The Negev Desert is in the south. It takes up more than half of Israel's land. Because there is so much desert area, water is a problem. The government built a system called the National Water Carrier. Giant pipes, canals, and tunnels move water from the Sea of Galilee to cities and desert areas in the south. This sea is really a large freshwater lake.

On the map, look at the eastern boundary of Israel. All along the boundary is the Great Rift Valley. It is millions of years old. The valley is

*The Jordan River in the north of Israel.*

a deep split in the earth's crust. The Jordan River is also here. It is the largest river in Israel. It flows into the Dead Sea, which is very salty. It is the lowest place on the earth.

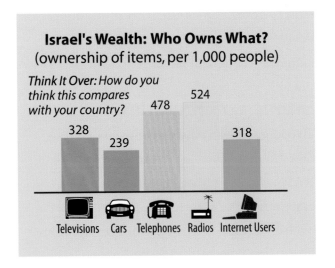

**Israel's Wealth: Who Owns What?**
(ownership of items, per 1,000 people)

*Think It Over: How do you think this compares with your country?*

Televisions 328
Cars 239
Telephones 478
Radios 524
Internet Users 318

71

**Population Distribution Map of Israel 2007**

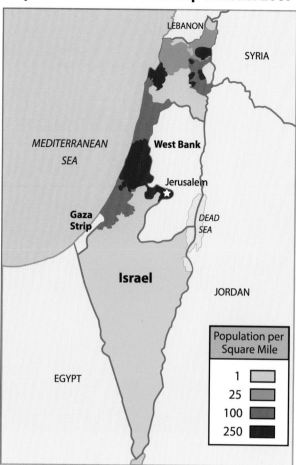

People come from many different countries. They speak many different languages. The government set up language classes for everyone. They teach Hebrew.

**Ethnic Divisions of Israel**

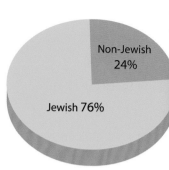

Arabs make up another major ethnic group. They speak Arabic. Most Arabs are **Muslims**. Two Arab groups play an important role in Israel's culture. They are the Bedouin and the Druze. Some Bedouin tribes are **nomads.** They move with their herds of animals from place to place. The Druze are mostly farmers.

# The Many Communities of Israel

Israel's communities are a mix of different peoples and ways of life. Jews, Arabs, and Christians all live in Israel.

## Ethnic Communities

Two large Jewish **ethnic groups** live in Israel. One group is called the Ashkenazim (ahsh-kuh-NAH-zuhm). They are Jews from northern and eastern Europe. The second group is called the Sephardim (suh-FAHR-duhm). They are from Spain, Iran, Yemen, and North Africa.

*A Bedouin rides a camel and talks on his satellite phone.*

72

## Activity

**Use the map on page 70 to answer questions 1–3.**

**1.** Name the four countries that border Israel.

a. _____     c. _____

b. _____     d. _____

**2.** Use the map on page 70 and the Population Distribution Map on page 72. Why do you think the population density is low in the south of Israel?

_____

_____

**3.** Based on information from the map, why are so many cities located on the west coast of Israel?

_____

**4.** Water is important in a desert environment. Describe how Israel brings water to cities and desert areas in the south.

_____

_____

# Religious Communities

In 1948, Palestine became Israel. It became a homeland for Jewish people. Arab Palestinians and other Arab countries were against this new nation. Today, these groups still argue over who owns the land.

About 76% of the country's population is Jewish. **Judaism** is one of the world's oldest major religions. It teaches the belief in one God. The Torah is Judaism's sacred book. It teaches Jewish history. It also teaches the laws of Judaism. The Jewish house of worship is called a **synagogue**.

**Muslims** make up the next largest religious group. They are followers of **Islam**. It teaches the belief in one God called Allah in Arabic. Islam was founded by Muhammad. He is called

**Major Religions of Israel**

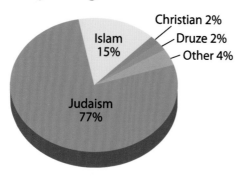

- Christian 2%
- Druze 2%
- Other 4%
- Islam 15%
- Judaism 77%

Allah's **prophet**, or messenger. The Koran is their holy book. Their house of worship is called a **mosque.**

A small group of people are Christian. They are followers of Jesus. The Bible is their sacred book. Thousands of Christians travel to Israel each year. They come to celebrate religious events, such as Easter. Others come to see where Jesus lived, taught, and died.

# Artistic and Cultural Communities

Art is everywhere in Israel. There are museums and parks. Small, colorful **mosaic** tiles decorate Muslim mosques. Stained-glass windows glow in synagogues and churches.

Music and dance are important parts of Israel's culture. The people love music. They enjoy going to concerts and folk dances. Israelis

## At a Glance

### Holidays and Festivals

*Because Israel is a Jewish state, all Jewish holidays and festivals are national holidays.*

**Rosh Hashanah:** The Jewish New Year celebrated in the fall.

**Yom Kippur:** The most sacred Jewish holiday. Jews ask for the forgiveness of sins.

**Hanukkah:** An eight day "festival of lights," usually in December. Celebrated with lighted candles, gifts, special games, and traditional foods.

**Passover:** Spring Jewish freedom festival. A special family meal called a seder with traditional foods like matzo and bitter herbs.

**Independence Day:** Celebrates the establishment of the State of Israel. There are parades, fireworks, and concerts.

### ★Other Festivals

**Ramadan:** A Muslim holy period of prayer and fasting that lasts for one month.

*Families eat special foods at the Passover seder.*

(Top) The Al Aksa Mosque and the Godlen Dome of the Rock are seen above the Western Wall.
(Bottom) A farmer moves cartloads of apples.

also love to read. The country prints more books per person than almost anywhere else in the world.

## Daily Life

How people live in Israel depends on where they live. About 90% of the population lives in **urban** areas. Most city people work in business, **industry**, or the building trades. A small number of Israelis are farmers.

## Educational Communities

Education is very important in Israel. Most children go to pre-school. They go to school six days a week. There is only one day with no school. It is Friday, Saturday, or Sunday. The day depends on the student's religion.

Most children of different religions go to different schools. They all learn math, science, history, and reading. They also study their own religions and cultures. By the fifth grade, everyone studies English. After high school, most Jewish students have to serve in the Israeli army.

## Communities of Friends

Children in Israel enjoy sports. Their favorite sport is soccer. Scouting is also popular. Almost all Israeli boys and girls belong to a youth group. These groups go hiking and camping. They also work in community service programs helping people in need. Community centers also have after-school programs for children. Here kids can work on arts and craft projects.

## Family Communities

Family life is important in Israel. Friday evenings and Saturdays are special times for Jews. It is the Sabbath, which is a holy day of

 **Activity**

1. In 2005, Israelis let the Palestinian rule Gaza. How might turning over this area of land help create peace in Israel?

   _____

   _____

2. Several cultures celebrate a festival of lights. What is the name of the Jewish festival of lights?

   _____

3. Why do you think both Hebrew and Arabic are official languages in Israel?

   _____

4. Each major religion has a sacred book. List the three sacred books of Judaism, Islam, and Christianity.

   Judaism: _____

   Islam: _____

   Christianity: _____

rest. Buses do not run. Stores and businesses are closed. Most Jewish families have a special meal together. The meal includes lighting candles. Some families attend religious services.

During holidays and school vacations, Israeli families explore their country. Many go camping, have picnics, or visit ancient buildings and ruins.

*(Top right) The church of the Holy Sepulcher in Jerusalem was built in 335 A.D. (Bottom left) A scribe copies the Torah. (Bottom right) Jewish Orthodox boy.*

# Jerusalem

Jerusalem is the capital of Israel. It is a holy city to three religions. These are Judaism, Islam, and Christianity. The city has been fought over many times. This is very sad because Jerusalem means "the city of peace."

Jerusalem has two parts. The eastern part is called The Old City. The Old City is surrounded by ancient stone walls. It is divided into four "quarters": Jewish, **Muslim**, Christian, and Armenian.

*A woman washes clothes in an ancient pool inside the walls of Old Jerusalem.*

## Learn a Skill

### Understand a Photograph

**Photographs** tell us about people, places, and events. They tell a story without words. First, look for the main idea or subject in a photograph. What is happening in the photograph? Next, look at the people, objects, and activities. Ask yourself what story the photographer is trying to tell you.

The Western Wall, or "Wailing Wall," is in the area called the Temple Mount. This is the holiest site for Jews. Near the Western Wall is the blue and gold Dome of the Rock. This **mosque** is one of the holiest sites for Muslims. Also in the Old City is the Church of the Holy Sepulcher, a very holy place for Christians.

The Old City is very busy. There is activity from morning to night. Visitors come from all over the world. Some shop in the open-air markets. Others visit holy sites.

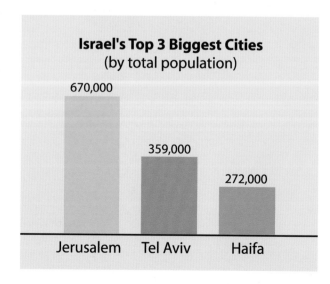

**Israel's Top 3 Biggest Cities**
(by total population)

|  |  |
| --- | --- |
| Jerusalem | 670,000 |
| Tel Aviv | 359,000 |
| Haifa | 272,000 |

## Activity

**Apply Understand a Photograph.** Your teacher will give you an Analyze a Photograph organizer. Look at the photograph of the family seder on page 74. Fill out the organizer. Then answer questions 1–3.

**1.** What is the photograph about?

_____

**2.** What are the people doing in the photograph?

_____

_____

**3.** Name two items that you see on the table.

_____

*Vegetable sellers in the Muslim Quarter of Old Jerusalem.*

The western part of Jerusalem is called the New City. Most of it is modern. There are museums, new shops, and tall office buildings. Israel's national government buildings are located here.

The Knesset is like the United States Congress in Washington, D.C. The Knesset is the government building where Israel's laws are made.

## Learn a Skill

**Charts** help you organize and classify information. This makes it easier to understand what you have read.

## An Old and New City

Here comes the bus! It stops in front of your hotel, the famous King David Hotel. The hotel is made of pink sandstone. You hop on board. The driver greets you. Then you're off to explore Jerusalem.

Jerusalem is built on many hills. The buildings are located on the hilltops. The valleys have parks and recreation areas.

Your first stop is Mt. Scopus. This mountain has a magnificent view of the Old City. In ancient times, Romans and Christian soldiers attacked Jerusalem from this place.

The bus stops at the Hadassah Medical Center. In the Medical Center's synagogue, you visit the famous Chagall stained-glass windows. The famous French artist Marc Chagall made

*Israel's Parliament, or Knesset, is located in the new part of Jerusalem.*

*People shop in the Muslim Quarter of Old Jerusalem.*

these twelve windows. They were a gift to Israel. Each window shows pictures of Jewish history.

The bus takes you to the Jaffa Gate. A walking trip is the best way to see the Old City. The Old City is less than a mile square. The streets are very narrow. Just inside the gate is the Christian Quarter. You look up at the Church of the Holy Sepulcher. Christians believe that Jesus died and was buried at this site.

The main shopping area in the Muslim Quarter is nearby. In the crowded souk (market), Arab shopkeepers call to you. They sell food, clothing, jewelry, and crafts. You walk along crooked streets that are three thousand years old!

You pass through the Armenian and Jewish Quarters. Then enter the Western Wall square. Many Jews stand at the wall. Some push small pieces of paper into holes in the wall. These papers contain written prayers.

**Four Quarters of the Old City in Jerusalem**

Now you leave the Old City. It is a short bus ride to the modern New City. You ride up a hilltop to visit the Knesset. A shopping mall is nearby. You are ready for some evening shopping. Then you remember! It's Friday. Because of the Jewish holy day, buses do not run from sunset on Friday to sunset on Saturday. So you hurry back on the bus for the trip back to the King David Hotel.

## Activity

**1.** What three major religions call Jerusalem a holy city?

a. _____

b. _____

c. _____

**2.** List one way the Knesset in Jerusalem is like the Congress in the United States.

_____

_____

**3. Apply Use Charts to Classify Information.** Study the list of words and places below that appear in this chapter. Then classify the list by its relationship to a religious tradition. Fill in the columns to complete the chart.

| | | |
|---|---|---|
| Wailing Wall | church | Dome of the Rock |
| Ramadan | Easter | Church of the Holy Sepulcher |
| synagogue | Hannukah | mosque |

| Judaism | Islam | Christianity |
|---|---|---|
| | | |
| | | |
| | | |

# Chapter 8
# South Africa

**How Big?** South Africa is almost twice the size of Texas.

Can you guess where South Africa is located? Its name gives you a clue. South Africa is located at the southern tip of Africa. The **continent** of Africa is huge. South Africa is south of the **equator.** That means it is in the **Southern Hemisphere.** Seasons in the Southern Hemisphere are opposite of those in the **Northern Hemisphere.** When it is summer in the United States, South Africa has winter. South Africa shares its borders with the countries of Namibia, Botswana, Zimbabwe, Mozambique, Swaziland, and Lesotho. Find Lesotho on the map. It is a tiny kingdom surrounded by the country of South Africa.

Two bodies of water border South Africa. The Indian Ocean lies along the eastern coast. The South Atlantic Ocean lies along the western coast. Most of the land in South Africa is made up of **plateaus.** The people call them **velds.** These are grassy plains. The five African "big-game

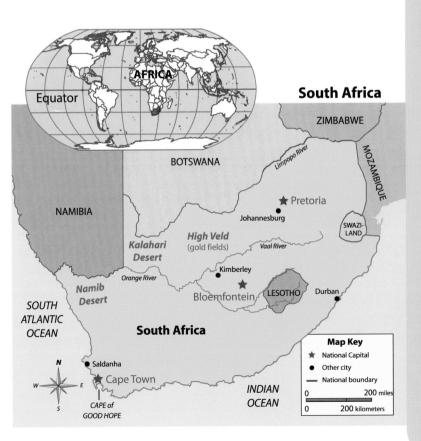

## At a Glance

**Official name:** Republic of South Africa

**Capitals:** Pretoria (executive); Cape Town (legislative) Bloemfontein (judicial)

**Area:** 471,011 square miles (1,219,912 sq km)

**Population:** 43,997,828

**Form of government:** Republic

**Chief crops:** corn, wheat, sugarcane, fruits, vegetables, beef, poultry, mutton, wool, dairy products

**Major industries:** mining, automobile assembly, metalworking, machinery, textiles, iron and steel, chemicals, fertilizer, foodstuffs, ship repair

**Natural resources:** world's largest producer of platinum, gold, chromium; coal, iron ore, natural gas, manganese, nickel, phosphates, tin, uranium, diamonds, copper, salt

43% rural
57% urban

**Population Distribution**

**Basic unit of money:** Rand (ZAR). One rand is equal to about $0.15 US cents.

**Main languages:** 11 official languages including Xhosa, Afrikaans, English, Setswana, Sesotho

**Major religions:** Christianity, Islam, traditional beliefs

83

**South Africa's Wealth: Who Owns What?**
(ownership of items, per 1,000 people)

*Think It Over: How do you think this compares with your country?*

355
138
90
108
68

Televisions  Cars  Telephones  Radios  Internet Users

animals" live on these plains. These are lions, buffalo, rhinos, hippos, and elephants. Many other animals also live here.

The world's largest and richest gold fields are in an area called the High Veld. Gold, diamonds, and other metals are South Africa's most important natural resources. Many people work in the mines and factories.

South Africa gets little rain. This makes the land better for **grazing** animals than for farming. South Africa is one of the main producers of sheep and wool.

The **fertile** areas along the coasts are narrow. Large parts of the country are desert. The Namib Desert runs along the west coast. The great Kalahari Desert is in the north.

# Activity

1. **Look at the map and the map key on page 83.** Which capital is located the farthest north in South Africa?

   _____

2. Using the map, which country shares a border with South Africa on the west coast?

   _____

3. Christmas and New Year's Day come during the summer in South Africa. From your reading, explain why this happens.

   _____

   _____

4. Look at the bar graph above. Which two items have less ownership than telephones in South Africa?

   a. _____    b. _____

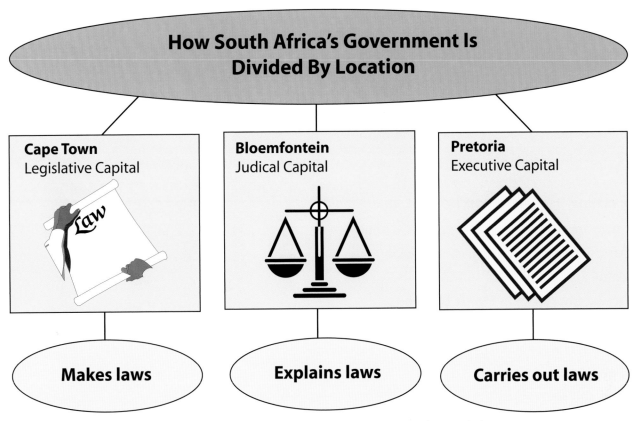

## How South Africa's Government Is Divided By Location

**Cape Town**
Legislative Capital

**Bloemfontein**
Judical Capital

**Pretoria**
Executive Capital

Makes laws

Explains laws

Carries out laws

*This diagram shows how South Africa divides the powers of the government among three capitals. Each capital city has its own responsibility for the laws of the land.*

# The Many Communities of South Africa

From 1948 until 1994, South Africa had a government policy called **apartheid** (uh-PAHR-tayt). Apartheid means "apartness" in the Afrikaans language. These laws told black people where they could live. Laws told them what jobs they could have. Laws even told them whom they could marry.

The government separated whites and blacks. It set up

*Cape Town is surrounded by mountains. It borders the South Atlantic Ocean.*

separate schools, restaurants, and other places. Slowly, South Africa began to change apartheid laws. In 1994, black South Africans voted for the first time. They elected Nelson Mandela, a black leader. He became the president of South Africa. Mandela had spent 26 years in prison for fighting against apartheid.

## Ethnic Communities

There are four major **ethnic groups** in South Africa. The country also has 11 official languages. The largest group is black, or African. It is shown on the pie graph as Black/African 79%. Different peoples make up this piece of the pie. The

**Ethnic Divisions of South Africa**

East Indian/Asian 2%
Colored 9%
White 10%
Black/African 79%

largest group is the Zulu. Other groups include the Xhosa and the Sotho. They speak the language of their own group. Many Africans also speak English.

The second-largest ethnic group is white. Most white South Africans are called Afrikaners. Their **ancestors** came from Europe. Many came from the Netherlands, France, and Germany. They speak Afrikaans. It is a mix of Dutch and African languages.

The third ethnic group is colored. They are a mix of native Africans, Asians, and white European races. Most of them speak Afrikaans. The last group is East Indian. They usually speak English and Hindi.

## Religious Communities

Most of the people in South Africa are Christians. On the pie graph, Christians make up 85% of the population. Whites, colored, and more than half of black Africans go to many

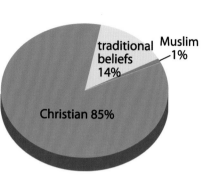

**Major Religions of South Africa**

traditional beliefs 14%
Muslim 1%
Christian 85%

different Christian churches. About 14% of black Africans follow **traditional** African religions.

*Nelson Mandela, first black African president of South Africa.*

86

## Artistic and Cultural Communities

Black South Africans have a rich **tradition** of folk arts and crafts. Their art is colorful. Each ethnic group has its own style. Artists use different materials. Some of these are beads, feathers, grass, clay, and wood. Artists make pottery, carvings, clothing, and jewelry.

The San people live in the Namib Desert. They are known for ancient rock and cave paintings of animals. Zulu women make beautiful jewelry. They use beads to make colorful patterns. The women also weave grass baskets. The men and boys carve wooden animals.

Traditional music and dance combines songs and storytelling. Musicians play drums,

## At a Glance

### Holidays and Festivals

#### ★National Holidays

**Freedom Day:** April 27. Celebrates the official end of apartheid. A new constitution was approved. Black South Africans voted for the first time.

#### ★Other Holidays

**Republic Day:** May 31. Marks the decision by white South African voters to be a republic rather than part of the British Empire.

**New Year's Day:** Celebrated as it is in the United States and other Western countries.

**Christmas and Easter:** Celebrated as it is in the United States and other Western countries.

**Grahamstown Festival:** Artists present music, theater, opera, and dance during this weeklong festival in July.

**Nagmaal Festival:** An Afrikaner religious and social event. Afrikaners

come in from the farms to the cities and towns to go to church and visit with friends. It is like a country fair.

**Day of the Vow:** December 16. Remembers a war between Zulu warriors and Afrikaner settlers.

*A Zulu man wears an elaborate headdress.*

87

pipes, and xylophones. They use their voices to sound like other musical instruments.

Older people tell stories, folktales, and poems to their children and grandchildren. This is how a group passes their history and customs to the next generation.

## Daily Life

In 1994, apartheid ended. The government is working to make changes. But life is still hard for black South Africans.

## Educational Communities

In 1955, the government passed a law. It said that black children were not allowed to learn math or science. They also did not have to go to school. The schools for black students were very poor. There was often no heat or lights. Students had no books or supplies. White children had good schools. They were in nice neighborhoods.

Since apartheid ended, schools are no longer separated by color. All children between the ages of 7 to 15 must go to school, or until they finish grade 9. The government spends a lot of money on education. But the problems from years of apartheid are hard to fix. In 2008, the government announced a list of free schools in poor, rural areas of the country. Forty percent of South African students go to these free schools. Poor parents do not pay for books and supplies. Schools in some black areas still do not have enough good teachers.

## Activity

1. Look at the diagram on page 85. Which capital in South Africa makes laws for the country?

   _____

2. Freedom Day is an important national holiday. It celebrates the end of apartheid. Why is it an important holiday for black South Africans?

   _____

   _____

3. Can you think of anything in United States history that was like apartheid? Explain.

   _____

   _____

*South Africa's children come from different backgrounds.*

## Communities of Friends

South Africans of all races love sports. The country's mild weather allows children to play outside most of the year. Swimming is popular. There are many swimming pools. They are open to everyone. Soccer and rugby are also favorite team sports. Scouting is also very popular with boys and girls. Scout troops work on projects to help people in the community.

## Family Communities

About two thirds of all white South Africans live in **urban** areas. The lives of most white families are much like middle-class Americans' lives. They own homes. They have nice cars. There is money for vacations. White adults still have the best jobs in government, business, and **industry**. About half of black South Africans lead western-style lives in urban townships or cities. Townships are crowded areas of small homes outside of cities.

### Learn a Skill

The **main idea**, or central issue, of a paragraph tells the most important idea about a paragraph. As you read, look for the main idea. It is often the first or second sentence. Look for facts and **details** that support the main idea. Look for an idea that all the sentences or paragraphs have in common.

(Top) Traditional Zulu houses are beehive-shaped grass huts. Most huts have no windows and only a doorway.
(Bottom) Mineworkers come up from the Harmony Gold Mine near Johannesburg.

But life for many black South Africans is still very hard. Many live in **rural** areas called homelands. It is hard to make a living. Some earn money by farming. Their houses are traditional cone-shaped dwellings. They are made of mud, grass, and straw. Fathers often leave their families for a long time. They work in mines and factories that are far away. Sometimes they can only come home to see their families once or twice a year.

## Activity

1. Study the photograph of traditional Zulu houses. Describe three ways that Zulu houses are different from houses in your community.

   a. _____

   b. _____

   c. _____

2. **Apply Main Idea.** Reread the second paragraph under the heading **Family Communities** on page 89. Circle the statement below that identifies the main idea of the paragraph.

   A. Rural areas of South Africa are called homelands.

   B. People make a living by farming.

   C. Houses are cone-shaped dwellings.

   D. Life is still hard for many black South Africans.

3. Apartheid has ended. Why are schools in many black areas still in very poor condition? Do you think these schools will change over time? Explain your answers.

   _____

   _____

   _____

# Johannesburg

Johannesburg is the largest city in South Africa. The city began more than 100 years ago. That's when gold was discovered nearby. Today, Johannesburg is the center of business, finance, and mining.

Johannesburg is a young, modern city. New office buildings rise up everywhere. The shopping malls are crowded. Families visit parks and museums. Art galleries, theaters, and restaurants are open late at night. Some **suburbs** have lovely homes. Wealthy white people live here. Other areas of Johannesburg are poor. Many black people who live here still live in shacks.

Fifteen miles outside Johannesburg is the **urban** township of Soweto. Apartheid laws created townships. In 1959, the government also set up **rural** "homelands." Millions of black South Africans had to leave their homes. They had to live in areas far away.

Black Africans could work in cities, but they could not live there. Today, most black South Africans still live in the townships.

More than two million people live in Soweto. This makes the township larger than the city of Johannesburg. Soweto is a mixture of poor areas and neighborhoods with more money. There are modern schools, shopping centers, and open-air markets. But parts of Soweto are large **slums**. Slums have cramped housing. They have no running water

*Women shop at a fruit stand in a Johannesburg market.*

*People in the Johannesburg township of Soweto line up to vote in their third election April 14, 2004.*

and no electricity. Trash is not taken away.

Almost half of the people in Johannesburg work in the gold mines. The mines are near the city. Some people work in businesses and factories. Factories in Johannesburg make chemicals, machinery, furniture, and cut diamonds.

## Take the "Freedom Trip"

Let's go on a "freedom trip." You will visit places that tell you about black South Africa's fight for freedom. Hop on a bus in downtown Johannesburg. Soon you are in the township of Soweto. On the way, you pass pale yellow hills. These "hills" are really piles of dirt from the city's oldest gold mines. These old mines are

## Learn a Skill

Writers do not always state the main idea directly. They want you to "read between the lines" to find the main idea. This is an **implied main idea.** To understand the main idea, you need to read the paragraph and think about the topic. Next, look at the details and facts. Then, write a statement that sums up the main idea. Here is a famous quotation from Nelson Mandela. *"When the water starts boiling, it is foolish to turn off the heat."* The main idea is that when black South Africans began to fight for their freedom, they should not stop until they win freedom.

93

*Two school boys in the township of Tsakane Brakpan play a game of cricket.*

now closed. Millions of black people worked in these mines. It was difficult and dangerous work. Many black workers were hurt or died.

Your first stop is Soweto. The township is changing. You drive by many neat and clean houses. They have flower and vegetable gardens. You see shops and schools. Nearby is one of the largest hospitals in South Africa. In other areas, you pass rows of shacks. There is no running water. Children fill jugs with water from a local pipe. There is no electricity. Trash is everywhere.

Next, you visit the Apartheid Museum. It shows the history of apartheid. There are photographs and films about black South

Africans fighting for their freedom. One photograph shows Nelson Mandela. He is receiving the Nobel Peace Prize. This special award was given to him for his work in ending apartheid.

**South Africa's Top 3 Biggest Cities**
(by total population)

| | | |
|---|---|---|
| 2.9 million | 2.7 million | 2.4 million |
| Cape Town | Johannesburg | Durban |

A few streets away is Nelson Mandela's house. During his fight against apartheid, government soldiers attacked his home. Later, this is where Nelson Mandela met world leaders. They came to see him after he became the president of South Africa.

Apartheid has ended. Much still needs to be done. But the people of South Africa continue to work to change their government and society.

*Students at the Sagewood Education Center in Johannesburg.*

## Activity

1. **Understand Implied Main Idea**. Read the paragraph below. It has a quotation by Nelson Mandela. Write the implied main idea of the quotation. Remember to "read between the lines."

   Apartheid kept whites in control of the country. During the 1950s and 1960s, blacks protested against it. Hundreds of people were wounded or killed by the police. Each small step toward freedom was a hard fight. Mandela said, "After climbing a great hill, one only finds that there are many more hills to climb."

   _____

   _____

2. Study the photograph of voters in Soweto on page 93. Write one detail in the photograph that tells you voting was important to the people in Soweto.

   _____

   _____

95

*Bryan Habana and the South Africa Springbok team beat England for the 2007 Rugby World Cup.*

## Activity

Apartheid created many problems for South Africa. Now that apartheid is over, there are still many problems. What do you think are some of the biggest problems facing South Africa today? Write about two problems that need to be solved.

a. _____

_____

b. _____

_____

# Chapter 9
# Puerto Rico

**How Big?** Puerto Rico is about the size of Connecticut.

If you live in the southern part of the United States, Puerto Rico is not far away. The small island is only 1,000 miles southeast of Florida. Puerto Rico is just a little smaller than the state of Connecticut. About 4 million people live there.

When you visit Puerto Rico, you have not really left the United States. Puerto Ricans are U.S. citizens. But Puerto Rico is not a U.S. state. It is a U.S. **commonwealth.** A commonwealth is a territory that belongs to another nation. The United States protects Puerto Rico. It gives aid to Puerto Rican citizens. Puerto Ricans can live, work, and travel in the United States. But Puerto Ricans who live on the island cannot vote in presidential elections.

Puerto Rico is north of the **equator.** That means it is in the **Northern Hemisphere.** It is part of an **archipelago** (ar-kuh-PEL-uh-goh)**,** or a group of small islands. This group is called the West Indies. It is more than 2,000 miles long. It lies in the Caribbean Sea between North and South America.

Most of the islands are the tops of mountains under the sea. Volcanoes formed these islands. Some are still active. Other islands are made of shells called coral. Look at the map below. North of Puerto Rico is the Atlantic Ocean.

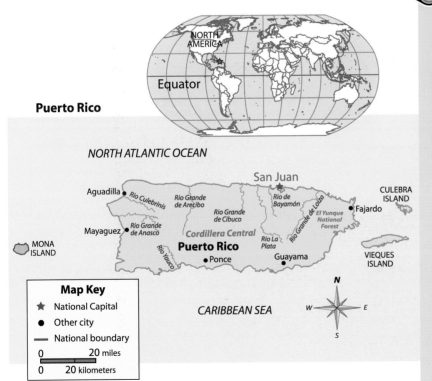

## At a Glance

**Official name:** Commonwealth of Puerto Rico
**Capital:** San Juan
**Area**: 3,508 square miles (9,085 km)
**Population:** 3,944,259
**Form of government:** Commonwealth associated with the United States
**Chief crops:** sugarcane, coffee, pineapples, plantains, bananas
**Major industries:** pharmaceuticals, electronics, apparel, food products, tourism
**Natural resources:** some copper and nickel; potential for some offshore and onshore crude oil
**Unit of money:** US dollar
**Main languages:** Spanish, English
**Major religions:** Roman Catholicism, Protestantism

29% rural
71% urban

**Population Distribution**

*Puerto Rico is an island that is protected by the United States.*

South of the island is the Caribbean Sea. The Virgin Islands and the Dominican Republic are Puerto Rico's nearest neighbors.

Tiny Puerto Rico has many different landforms. A long, flat belt of lowland runs along the north and south coasts. It is about ten miles wide. Large cities grew up in these areas. There are farms and sandy beaches. Millions of visitors come to the beaches each year. Tourism is a very important **industry** on the island.

Hills rise from the lowland towards rugged mountains. A long, narrow mountain range runs from west to east. It is in the center of Puerto Rico. The mountain range is called the Cordillera (kor-duhl-YUHR-uh) Central. Farmers grow coffee on the mountain slopes. They grow fruit in the valleys. No snow falls in Puerto Rico. Not even on the mountaintops.

The mountains in the northeast have the only tropical rain forest in the United States. This national forest is called El Yunque (el YOON-kay). About 200 inches of rain a year can fall in this small area.

Puerto Rico is often in the path of hurricanes. Hurricane season runs from June through November. Storms bring strong winds and heavy rains. They cause floods. Hurricanes also destroy homes, farms, and businesses.

# The Many Communities of Puerto Rico

Puerto Ricans belong to many different communities. Because the island is a U.S. commonwealth, large communities of Puerto Ricans live in the United States. Most make their homes in New York City.

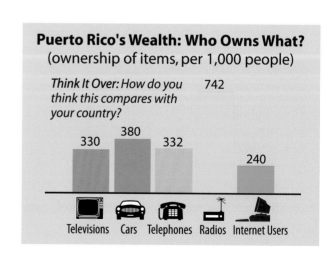

**Puerto Rico's Wealth: Who Owns What?**
(ownership of items, per 1,000 people)

*Think It Over: How do you think this compares with your country?*

Televisions 330, Cars 380, Telephones 332, Radios 742, Internet Users 240

98

*Police in Puerto Rico help people in Arecibo escape from floods. Hurricanes are a problem in the Caribbean.*

## Ethnic Communities

Most Puerto Ricans are a mix of different backgrounds. Their families came from European, African, and Native American **ethnic groups**. Most Puerto Ricans are also of Spanish **descent**. Their **ancestors** were Spanish settlers.

In 1493, Christopher Columbus claimed Puerto Rico for Spain. Thousands of Spanish settlers soon arrived. The settlers brought the Spanish language. They also brought their religion, Roman Catholicism. Spain ruled Puerto Rico for over 400 years.

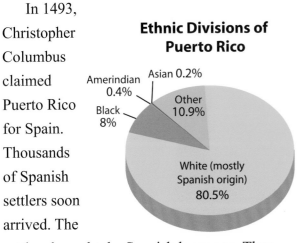

**Ethnic Divisions of Puerto Rico**

Asian 0.2%
Amerindian 0.4%
Black 8%
Other 10.9%
White (mostly Spanish origin) 80.5%

Many Spanish settlers married native people called the Taino. Other settlers married African slaves. In Puerto Rico, African slaves worked on Spanish plantations. These large Spanish farms grew coffee, sugar cane, and tobacco. In 1873, Spain ended slavery in Puerto Rico.

Later, Spain let other ethnic groups come to Puerto Rico. People from China came to work on the railroads. Workers from Lebanon, Italy, and the United States also came to Puerto Rico. People from other islands in the West Indies came to escape wars.

## Religious Communities

Almost all Puerto Ricans are Christians. Religion is very important. About 15% of the population belongs to Protestant religions. The rest of the people belong to the Roman Catholic religion. It was brought to Puerto Rico by the Spanish. Catholics have many customs, beliefs, and traditions based on their faith. They believe in the teachings of Jesus Christ and the writings in the Bible.

Many Catholic homes have pictures or statues of saints. They help and protect the family.

Some Puerto Ricans also have Indian and African beliefs. They practice spiritualism, or the belief in spirits. Spiritualists believe that some people have special powers. They can

**Major Religions of Puerto Rico**

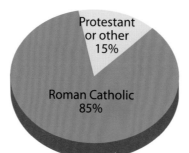

Protestant or other 15%

Roman Catholic 85%

heal sick people. They can also tell the future. **Rural** areas still practice traditional Indian and African ceremonies. They carry charms to keep away evil spirits.

## Artistic and Cultural Communities

Puerto Rico is famous for its music. Traditional Puerto Rican music has Taino, Spanish, and African roots.

African rhythms, or beats, are heard in music called salsa. Salsa means "sauce." It refers to salsa's "spicy," hot sound. Tito Puente

## At a Glance

### Holidays and Festivals

★**Religious Holidays**

**Las Navidades (Christmas):** December 25. Celebrated with church attendance, a feast with special foods, gift giving, and surprise visits to friends.

**Three Kings' Day:** January 6. Children receive gifts in exchange for the small boxes of grass they have left for the horses of the Three Wise Men.

**Feast of San Juan Bautista:** June 23. Celebrated with a picnic at the beach and a re-creation of the baptism of Jesus Christ. Honors St. John the Baptist, the island's patron saint.

**Feast of Santiago Apostol:** July 25. Celebrated with a parade of masked and costumed dancers. Honors St. James the Apostle.

★**Other Festivals**

**Pablo Casals Festival:** Spring. Established by the famous cellist whose mother was Puerto Rican. Celebrates classical music.

*A young boy wears a mask and costume for the Festival of Santiago Apostol.*

100

(phoo-EHN-tay), a Puerto Rican American, made salsa music popular in the United States. Classical music in Puerto Rico began with the famous cellist Pablo Casals. He started a music school, an orchestra, and a music festival.

## Daily Life

Daily life in Puerto Rico has changed over the last 50 years. Most people lived and worked in farming villages. Now, most people live in cities and **urban** areas.

## Word Watch

Did you know that the words *hurricane* and *hammock* come from Puerto Rico? The word *hurricane* comes from *hurakán*, the Taino word meaning "god of storm." The word *hammock* comes from *hamaca*, the Taino style of bed.

## Activity

**Use the map on page 97 to answer questions 1–2.**

1. Find the bodies of water north and south of the island. Why do you think Puerto Rico is often called a Caribbean island?

   _____

2. Look at the map and map scale. Which direction would you travel to go from Guayama to San Juan? _____ About how many miles would you travel? _____

3. What two changes to native culture did Spanish settlers bring to Puerto Rico?

   a. _____

   b. _____

4. Explain why Puerto Ricans might practice African or Native American spiritual beliefs along with their Christian religion.

   _____

   _____

**101**

## Educational Communities

In 1898, Spain and the United States fought the Spanish-American War. Puerto Rico became a U.S. territory. The U.S. government built schools, hospitals, and roads. At that time, few people could read. Now, 94% of the population over 15 years old can read and write. Their school system is like the U.S. system. But Puerto Rican students learn their lessons in Spanish. English is a second language.

## Communities of Friends

Baseball and basketball are popular sports. Children play baseball on neighborhood fields. Many baseball programs began because of Roberto Clemente. He is the island's most famous baseball hero. And, of course, water sports are popular. Puerto Rico is an island, so beaches are always close by. People go swimming and surfing.

Everyone enjoys going to festivals. Each town organizes one to honor its patron saint. There is usually a fairground with food, rides, and parades. Music and dancing are also part of the fun.

## Family Communities

Puerto Rican families have strong ties. Grandparents, parents, uncles, aunts, and children all do things together. Children are very important. There is an important family custom in Puerto Rico. Each child has a *compadre* (godfather) or *comadre* (godmother). The godparents are usually family friends.

They are treated with great respect. They are part of the family. Godparents may even bring up a child.

When Puerto Ricans move to the cities, they stay close to their relatives in the country. On weekends and vacations, people often visit their relatives in the country.

*Two young students from Abraham Lincoln Elementary School in San Juan.*

102

## Learn a Skill

**Political cartoons** are drawings. They make people think about events that are happening. The artist gives his or her point of view in the drawing. Cartoons often use words or symbols to explain their ideas. The political cartoon below was published in 1898. At that time, many people thought that Puerto Rico should become part of the United States. They believed the island was important to U.S. security. In the cartoon, the little girl stands for Puerto Rico. The wolf is also a symbol. It stands for other nations. The artist believed that the United States would protect Puerto Rico from other nations.

*A wolf barks at Puerto Rico in this political cartoon. In 1898, Puerto Rico asks for admission to the United States. Cartoon by A.W. Rogers.*

## Activity

1. **Apply Understand Political Cartoons.** Study the cartoon on page 103 to answer questions 1–2.

   a. Who is the little girl in the cartoon on page 103? _____

   b. Why do you think the artist uses a fierce wolf as a symbol for other nations?

   _____

   _____

2. Based on this cartoon, what is the artist saying about how the United States can help Puerto Rico?

   _____

   _____

   _____

   _____

3. What important family relationship in Puerto Rico helps families and children?

   _____

4. You learned that Puerto Rico is a commonwealth. What benefits did the United States bring to the people of Puerto Rico after the Spanish-American War?

   _____

   _____

   _____

# San Juan

San Juan is Puerto Rico's capital city. It is also the center of business and culture. A third of the island's population lives here. Millions of tourists visit San Juan every year.

San Juan is really two cities in one. Old San Juan is located on an island. Several bridges and a highway connect Old San Juan to the mainland. Narrow, winding streets lead to quiet plazas, or squares. There are ancient church **steeples** and powerful military **forts**. Spanish soldiers built them hundreds of years ago. The most famous reminder of Spanish rule is the huge fort on San Juan bay. It is called El Morro. It is one of Puerto Rico's most-recognized landmarks.

The *Condado* area is the business center of San Juan. It is very different from the feeling of old Spanish San Juan. There are high-rise hotels on the edge of busy beaches. Modern office buildings and fine stores crowd the streets.

Tourists and buses fill the busy streets. San Juan is also one of the busiest **ports** in the West Indies.

The Commonwealth of Puerto Rico is a territory of the United States. In the past, the U.S. government has asked Puerto Ricans to vote. They had to decide if they wanted to become a state or become an independent nation. Each time, Puerto Rican voters decided to stay as a commonwealth.

*High-rise buildings and hotels line San Jaun's sandy beaches.*

105

# In Old San Juan

Your ship has just docked in the old **port** city of San Juan. The sky is a deep blue. The air is warm. You begin a walking tour of Old San Juan. You soon see that the city was built as a **fort**. Two Spanish forts protect San Juan. El Morro guards the harbor. It rises 140 feet above the sea. You stop to explore the many underground tunnels and dungeons. Spanish soldiers used to train in the large field in front of El Morro. Now it is a picnic area. It is also a great place to fly kites.

The streets are paved with interesting blue stones. They came from old Spanish galleons, or ships. All around you are hundreds of Spanish-style buildings. They are bright colors of pink, peach, and coral.

*Young folk dancers wear traditional clothing.*

## Learn a Skill

When you **compare and contrast,** you see how things are alike and how they are different. In the diagram below, you learn how different kinds of government could affect the people of Puerto Rico. For example, as a state, Puerto Ricans could vote for the U.S. president, but they would have to pay U.S. federal taxes. As a commonwealth, they pay nothing. No one knows what the taxes might be as an independent nation.

| Three Kinds of Governments for Puerto Rico | | |
|---|---|---|
| **As the U.S. 51st State** | **As a Commonwealth** | **As an Independent Nation** |
| U.S. Citizen <br> • vote for U.S. President <br> • pay U.S. federal taxes <br> • languages English/Spanish | U.S. Citizen <br> • do not vote for U.S. President <br> • do not pay U.S. federal taxes. <br> • Spanish/English | Puerto Rican Citizen <br> • elect own president <br> • pay their own taxes <br> • Spanish |

The second fort you visit is San Cristóbal. It guards the city from attacks by land. You decide to have a picnic near the palm trees. The streets are very narrow. They go up steep hills. After a long walk in the old town, you are ready for a cooling swim. Palm trees grow along the sandy beaches. A short distance west of San Juan is the popular beach at Isla Verde.

Suddenly, church bells ring all over the city. It is the afternoon of

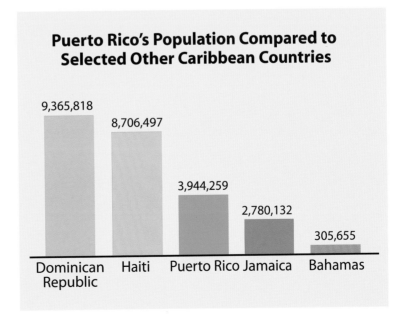

**Puerto Rico's Population Compared to Selected Other Caribbean Countries**

Dominican Republic: 9,365,818
Haiti: 8,706,497
Puerto Rico: 3,944,259
Jamaica: 2,780,132
Bahamas: 305,655

*An ancient wall surrounds Old San Juan. Military rulers lived at the Casa Blanca. It stands on top of the ancient wall that surrounds Old San Juan.*

July 23. All the shops and businesses are closed. Today is the feast of San Juan Bautista. He is the patron saint of San Juan.

You join the crowd hurrying to the beach. There is going to be big beach party! There is salsa music playing and everyone is dancing.

There is plenty of food. You try a hot *surullito* (sooh-reh-HEE-toh). It is a popular fried cornmeal snack. At midnight, you watch as local people greet the saint by walking backwards to the sea. Too soon it's time to return to your ship in the harbor!

*A woman cooks traditional Puerto Rican foods in a roadside restaurant.*

## Activity

**1.** What two forts protected Old San Juan?  a. _____

b. _____

**2. Apply Compare and Contrast.** Based on the information in the diagram on page 107, why might Puerto Rican voters decide to remain a commonwealth?

_____

_____

**3.** Puerto Rico means "rich port" in Spanish. It was the original name of San Juan. Now it means the whole island. Why do you think this might be a good name for Puerto Rico?

_____

_____

# Chapter 10
# Brazil

Your plane is about to land in Brazil. As you fly over, you can see a rain forest. Then you see swamps and grasslands. Snow covers mountain tops. Do not miss those gleaming beaches. There are miles and miles of coastline.

Most of Brazil is south of the **equator**. That means it is in the **Southern Hemisphere**. A small part of the country is above the equator. So a small part is in the **Northern Hemisphere**. Brazil is on the **continent** of South America. To the east, Brazil bumps out into the Atlantic Ocean. The country is big. In fact, the only countries in South America that do not border Brazil are Chile and Ecuador.

Most of Brazil's native people moved around the country. They fished, hunted, and gathered wild plants. Many formed villages. Some of these had as many as 5,000 people.

Brazil

Map Key
★ National Capital
● Other city
— National boundary
0  400 miles
0  400 kilometers

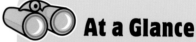

## At a Glance

**Official name:** Federative Republic of Brazil
**Capital:** Brasília
**Area:** 3,265,077 square miles (8,456,510 sq km)
**Population:** 186,112,794
**Form of government:** Federal republic
**Chief crops:** coffee, soybeans, wheat, rice, corn, sugarcane, oranges
**Major industries:** textiles, shoes, chemicals, cement, lumber, iron ore, autos and parts

17% rural
83% urban
**Population Distribution**

**Natural resources:** bauxite, gold, iron ore, chemicals, hydropower, timber
**Basic unit of money:** Real. One real is equal to about $0.58 US cents.
**Main languages:** Portuguese (official), Spanish, English, French
**Major religions:** None (official), Roman Catholic, Protestant

110

## Learn a Skill

Throughout this book, you see photos. These are **primary sources**. They were made at the time of an event. **Secondary sources** are materials that come from a later time. They are written or painted by people who did not personally experience an event. The artist of the painting below was not at the landing of Columbus.

In the 1400s, explorers from Spain and Portugal sailed the world. They were looking for new countries. Christopher Columbus landed on an island off the coast of Brazil. He claimed the land for Spain.

Soon Spain and Portugal were in a race to claim the land in South America. Pope

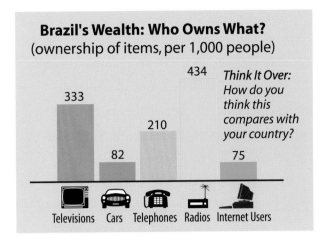

**Brazil's Wealth: Who Owns What?**
(ownership of items, per 1,000 people)

*Think It Over: How do you think this compares with your country?*

Televisions 333, Cars 82, Telephones 210, Radios 434, Internet Users 75

Alexander VI was the head of the Roman Catholic Church. He stepped into the fight between the countries.

In 1493, the pope drew an imaginary line around the world. It was called the Line of Demarcation. Spain got the lands west of the line. Portugal got the lands east of the line. This included eastern Brazil. This is why the people of Brazil speak Portuguese.

*Christopher Columbus landing in the Western Hemisphere. He claimed the land he found for Spain.*

111

Most of northern Brazil is covered by the Amazon rain forest. Find the Amazon River on the map on page 110. The river flows through this deep, wet forest. Manaus is one of the largest cities in this area. The rain forest is called the "lungs of the earth." It filters the earth's carbon dioxide gases.

But the rain forest is in trouble. Rain forests used to cover 14 percent of the earth's surface. Today, they cover only 6 percent. We are losing plants and animals. One and a half acres are lost every second. Lumbering is a major **industry**. People farm the land. This loss is probably changing our atmosphere and causing the earth to warm. People and governments are working to save the rain forests.

# The Many Communities of Brazil

More than half of all the people in South America live in Brazil. But much of Brazil is not very populated. Most people live near the coast. Only 7 percent of the people live in the huge Amazon region of Brazil. The population is a mix of whites, blacks, and Indians.

## Ethnic Communities

Most of the people in Brazil are of European **ancestry**. Most are **descended** from Portuguese settlers.

 **Activity**

**Apply secondary source.** Look at the painting on page 111. Your teacher will give you an organizer about how to analyze a painting. Fill out the organizer. Then answer the following questions.

1. What does the painting tell you about the explorers' religion?

_____

2. How are the native people shown in the painting?

_____

3. Why would people in Spain like this painting? Do you think what the painting shows is really true?

_____

# At a Glance

## Holidays and Festivals

### ★National Holidays

**New Year's Day:** January 1. Celebrated very much as it is in North America and other Western countries.

**Tiradentes Day:** April 21. Remembers the day that Joaquim José da Silva Xavier was executed. In 1789, he led an uprising for independence. *Tiradentes* means "tooth-puller." Xavier was a dentist.

**Labor Day:** May 1. Celebrated much as it is in the United States and elsewhere in the world.

**Independence Day:** September 7. Dom Pedro officially declared Brazil's independence from Portugal on this day in 1822.

**Day of the Republic:** November 15. This day celebrates the day in 1889 when Pedro II was removed from power.

### ★Religious Holidays

Most religious holidays are also national holidays.

**Carnival:** Late February or early March. This is the last fling before the serious pre-Easter season of Lent. Celebrations last 5 days. They end suddenly at midnight on the Tuesday before Ash Wednesday. This is the beginning of Lent, a time of fasting.

**Good Friday and Easter Sunday:** March/April. Celebrated as in other mostly Roman Catholic countries.

**Christmas:** December 25. Christmas in Brazil officially begins December 24. Remember, Brazil is in the Southern Hemisphere. That means it falls at the height of the summer season.

*The statue of Christ the Redeemer looks over the city of Rio de Janeiro. It stands about 120 feet high, and the arms are 92 feet from fingertip to fingertip. It weighs 700 tons. There is a small chapel inside the statue.*

**Ethnic Divisions
of Brazil**

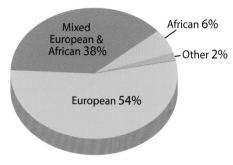

Mixed European & African 38%

African 6%

Other 2%

European 54%

are Roman Catholic. They are followers of Jesus Christ. The Bible is their sacred book. In the 1500s, priests from Portugal brought the Catholic faith to Brazil. Notice that many religious holidays in Brazil are also national holidays. Today, there are more Catholics in

*These samba dancers are dressed as colorful fish. They parade down the street during the Carnival festival in Rio de Janeiro.*

Other Europeans who settled in Brazil came from Germany, Russia, Spain, Italy, and Switzerland.

The second largest **ethnic group** is a mix of European and African ancestry. This group is shown on the pie graph as 38%.

**Descendants** of African slaves make up about 6 percent of Brazil's population. Brazil had brought over more African slaves than any other country in the world. This large country had huge sugar cane and coffee plantations. Finally in 1888, Brazil became the last nation in the Western Hemisphere to ban slavery. This group's ancestors came mostly from Nigeria, Angola, and the Congo.

# Religious Communities

There is no official religion in Brazil. But almost three quarters of Brazilians say they

**Major Religions of
Brazil**

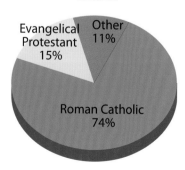

Evangelical Protestant 15%

Other 11%

Roman Catholic 74%

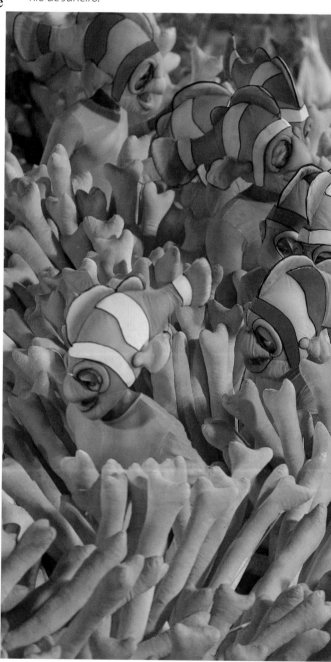

**114**

Brazil than in any other country in the world.

Many other Christians also live in Brazil. Evangelical Protestants make up 15 percent of the religions. Brazil also has Lutherans, Methodists, Anglicans, and Baptists. There are also smaller communities of Lebanese and Syrian. They follow **Islam**.

Candomblé is practiced by only about 0.3 percent of the people. Candomblé is a religion that mixes Catholic symbols and African beliefs. Slaves from West Africa brought the ideas with them to Brazil. People hold ceremonies at night, near a body of water. They sing, dance, beat drums, and call upon the gods.

## Artistic and Cultural Communities

Brazil has a rich **culture** of arts. Music, literature, and cinema have always been important. Brazilian culture is a mix of Native American, Portuguese, and African cultures.

Music and dancing are important. Brazil has many samba dancers. Like much of the music in Brazil, the samba began with African music and dance. In the 1950s, the bossa nova was born in Rio de Janeiro. It mixed jazz and offbeat rhythms. In 1963, the bossa nova became very popular in the United States.

## Activity

1. Why can most people in Brazil trace their ancestry to Portugal?

_____

2. Many of the religions, festivals, and holidays in Brazil include singing and dancing. Why do you think music is such an important part of celebrations in so many cultures? Explain your answer.

_____

_____

3. Why do you think Brazil brought over more enslaved Africans than any other country in the world?

_____

_____

*A Brazilian girl working in the classroom.*

The music of Heitor Villa-Lobos is based on Brazilian folk tunes. His work is popular all over the world.

Brazil is also home to many popular painters. The country also has many beautiful buildings. There are old opera houses and churches. There are also stunning modern buildings.

## Daily Life

Even though Brazil is a very large country, most people live in the cities. The largest cities are in the southeast. Why do Brazilians leave the open spaces to live in crowded cities? They are looking for better jobs, homes, and education. In cities, some people live in beautiful homes. Others live in terrible slums.

Some people do not live in large cities. Along the edge of the Amazon River, houses are built high off the ground on stilts. This protects homes from floods during the rainy season. The Amazon rain forest is still home to many indigenous (native) people. Even today, about 40 tribes live so far into the forest that they have no contact with outsiders.

Large parts of the north are covered with wet, tropical rain forests. In the northeast, there is little rain. The land is dry.

## Educational Communities

Schools are free in Brazil. All children between the ages of 7 and 14 must go to school. Children in Brazil go to school for four hours a day. They go to classes either in the morning or in the afternoon.

In Brazil, there are two types of high schools. Some high schools get students ready for college. Vocational schools get students ready for jobs.

There are many colleges and universities in Brazil. About half of these are private Catholic schools. The others are free public colleges. To go on to college, students have to take a national exam. Sadly, many students from public high schools cannot pass the exam. Public schools do

not get students ready for college. One-fifth of Brazilians cannot read or write.

## Communities of Friends

Brazilians are like most people all over the world. They love sports. Their national sport is soccer, called *futebol* in Brazil. Edson Arantes do Nascimento is better known as Pelé. Many think he was the best soccer player in the world. Led by Pelé, Brazil won the World Cup in 1958, 1962, and 1970.

Auto racing, volleyball, and basketball are also popular. Brazilians also love to play sports. There are many clubs for sports. People love to explore caves, climb mountains, water ski, and dive under water.

*Brazilians love* futebol *(soccer).* Pelé *is one of the most famous soccer players in the world.*

*Capoeira* is a mix of martial arts, dancing, and fighting. Schools that teach this sport are found throughout Brazil.

## Family Communities

Brazilians are friendly. Friends greet each other with handshakes, kisses, and hugs. Visitors are always welcome.

In the past, families in Brazil were very large. Today, many families are smaller, with 2 or 3 children. Three or four generations of a family often live in the same home. Families are very close. At holidays, there are often large family gatherings.

Brazilian food is a mix of the many cultures of Brazil. *Feijoada* (fey-zhoo-AH-dah) is the national dish. It is a wonderful stew. This mix of black beans, spices, sausage, and other meats is very heavy. You may need to take a nap after lunch.

*Churrasco* is a favorite in the south. Chunks of beef are grilled on long skewers. If you want something light, there are wonderful fruits and vegetables. Brazil's farm and grazing land is about twice the size of Texas. Don't forget about all that coastline. Brazilians also love fish.

Many middle-class Brazilians rent apartments in high-rise buildings. Others own homes in the suburbs. The upper class lives in very lovely, large homes. Many look like palaces. High fences surround the homes.

But every large city also has its *favelas* (fah-VEL-us). These are slums. People live with very little. They have no running water or sewers. Many do not have electricity.

 **Activity**

1. Reread the paragraphs about where people live in the cities. Think about a large city near where you live. List one way your city is like a city in Brazil. List one way it is different.

   **Same:** _____

   **Different:** _____

2. Most Brazilians live along the coast. The rest of the country is mostly unpopulated. List two reasons why people move to the cities.

   a. _____

   b. _____

3. Describe how your school day is different from a school day in Brazil.

   _____

   _____

   _____

118

# Brasília

Brasília was not always the capital of Brazil. The capital used to be Rio de Janeiro. Brasília was built far from any major city. The government hoped that people would move from the crowded coastal cities to the capital inland. In 1956, builders began work on the city. On April 21, 1960, Brasília opened as the capital. The city is well known for its **architecture.**

South of the Amazon region is the central **plateau.** Brazil's capital, Brasília, sits in the middle of this empty area. Outside of the city are large grassy **plains.** To the south is rich farmland. There are also plantations and cattle ranches.

Today, Brasília has a little over 3 million people. Government buildings are located in the city. Like the government in the United States, the government of Brazil has three branches. These are the legislative, executive, and judicial.

The legislative branch makes the laws. They meet in the National Congress Building. The executive branch carries out the laws and includes the president and vice president. The president and vice president must be born in Brazil. They also must be at least 35 years old.

*The modern city of Brasília. Construction began in 1956. In 1960, Brasília officially opened.*

*Waterfalls and pools in front of the National Congress Building.*

The third branch is the judiciary. This branch explains the laws. The highest court is the Supreme Federal Tribunal. It has eleven judges.

Brasília has an unusual design for a city. It is shaped like an airplane. The government offices form the center part of the plane. This is the part of the plane called the cabin. It has all the seats.

The "nose" of the plane has the Square of the Three Powers. Here sit the buildings for the three branches of government. The airplane's "wings" are made up of high-rise apartment buildings and businesses. In the "tail" of the plane sits the Senate, Palace of Justice, and the Presidential Palace.

In 1987, Brasília was added to the World Heritage Sites list. The list includes buildings and places that are important to save. Brasília is on the list for its bold urban planning and its exciting architecture.

## Welcome to Brasília

*Olá* means "hello." You will hear that very often in the city. The people are friendly. Get ready to see the sights. There will also be a tour to a famous waterfall.

The first stop on your tour of the city is the famous TV tower. The tower is 426 feet tall, and you will go to the very top. Here you get a bird's-eye view of the city. It really is shaped like an airplane.

### Learn a Skill

When you **take notes**, you write down important details and ideas from the chapter, paragraph, or passage you are reading. You can organize your notes by using graphic organizers, such as word webs, summary sheets, or outlines.

**120**

Because of the design, it is easy to find your way around the city. Next stop is the Memorial dos Povos. This building is shaped like a *maloca.* That is a tradition longhouse used by native people. It is a reminder of what the native people have added to Brazil's culture.

The buildings are amazing. They look like pieces of art. Some of the most exciting buildings are the churches. The national Cathedral is designed to look like a crown. Angels hang inside from the ceiling.

Most of the businesses here stay open all day. But some close from noon until about 2:00 p.m. for a long lunch break. You may want to stop by an open-air market and shop for dinner. Here you will find fresh vegetables, fruits, and beautiful flowers. You may be surprised by the number of different types of bananas. The ones from the Amazon area are round and sweet.

After dinner, get a good night's sleep. Tomorrow you are off on a four-day trip. You will go to Iguacu Falls. It is on the Brazil and

# Activity

**1.** Why did the Brazilian government move the capital from Rio de Janeiro to Brasília?

_____

_____

**2. Apply Taking Notes.** Reread the paragraphs about Brazil's government and its 3 branches. Complete the outline below by listing 3 details about Brazil's government.

**Three Branches of Brazil's Government**

A. Legislative

1._____

B. Executive

1._____

C. Judicial

1._____

*Like many big cities, Brasília has slums. More than 1 million of the city's population live in slums. More than 31 percent of Brazil's population lives in poverty.*

Argentina border. There are 275 waterfalls here. They tumble over a horseshoe-shaped rim. If you are brave, you may want to take a walk on the wooden sidewalks balanced on the edge of the thundering falls. It is one of South America's greatest natural sights!

## Activity

**1.** What is unusual about the design of Brasília?

_____

_____

**2.** Imagine that you have a student from Brazil visiting you. Write 4 interesting facts about the area in which you live. You may want to include information about landmarks, food, climate, and so on.

a. _____

b. _____

c. _____

d. _____

# Student Glossary

**ancestors/ancestry** Family and ethnic background; descent. Members of your family who lived long ago are your ancestors.

**apartheid** South Africa's past government policy that separated citizens by race.

**archipelago** An island chain made up of many islands near one another.

**architecture** Buildings and structures. High-rises, churches, and bridges make up the architecture of many cities.

**atheist** Someone who does not believe in God.

**Buddhism** A religion based on the teachings of an Indian wise man known as the Buddha.

**calligraphy** The art of fine writing. Chinese writing has many beautiful kinds of calligraphy.

**caste system** A system in India that divided people into groups based on their job and wealth.

**century** A time period of 100 years. 400 years is four centuries.

**chemical** A substance, usually made by people, created to do a specific function.

**citizens** People who are granted full rights under the government of a country. U.S. citizens can vote, get U.S. passports, and are protected by the Constitution.

**citrus** Kind of fruit with high acid content. Oranges and grapefruit are citrus fruits.

**climate** The average weather conditions of a region over a long period of time. The climate of most Caribbean islands is warm.

**colony** A place where a group of people come to settle that is under control of their home country. English settlers formed colonies in America in the 1600s.

**commonwealth** A self-governing state or nation that shares a common leadership or ruler. Puerto Rico is a commonwealth that is protected by the United States.

**Communism/Communist** A form of government in which one political group has complete control over daily life, including the country's economy.

**compass** A navigation tool that shows direction (north, south, east, and west).

**Confucianism** Ideas of an ancient Chinese teacher named Confucius that were practiced in China and other parts of Asia.

**continent** A large, continuous mass of land. The seven continents of the world are Asia, Australia, Antarctica, North American, South America, Africa, and Europe.

**culture** Customs, traditions, languages, or religion shared by a group of people or nation.

**democracy** A government by the people, where citizens control the power. The United States of America is a democracy.

**descendant/descent** Someone who is related by blood to a person from an older generation; family line. You are a descendant of your ancestors.

**equator** An imaginary line around the middle of the earth that separates the Northern Hemisphere from the Southern Hemisphere.

**ethnic group** A group of people that share the same racial, national, tribal, religious, or cultural background.

**evergreen** A kind of tree that does not lose its leaves in winter.

**fertile** Rich, productive. Fertile soil produces plentiful crops.

**fort/fortress** Walls and structures built for protection.

**geography** The study of the world. It explores people, places, and the land.

**graze** To feed upon the growth of a pasture or meadow. Cows graze in pastures.

**heritage** Ideas and beliefs that are passed on to families and cultural groups about their past.

**Hinduism** An ancient religion in India.

**human-environment interaction** Tells you how people and the environment affect each other; one of the five ideas that show how geography connects the world.

**immigrant** A person who comes to a new country to set up a life.

**industry** Major businesses.

**invent** Create something new. Fireworks were invented in China.

**Islam** A religion based on the teachings of the prophet Mohammed.

**Judaism** The religion of the Hebrews, based on a belief in one God.

**location** Tells you where a place is; one of the five ideas that show how geography connects the world.

**manufacturing** The process of taking raw materials and making them into finished goods.

**monarch** King or queen.

**mosaic** A design or image created with many small pieces of pottery or tile.

**mosque** An Islamic building for worship.

**movement** Tells how people, goods, and ideas get from place to place; one of the five ideas that show how geography connects the world.

**multicultural** Involving or made up of people from different races or religions.

**Muslim** A follower of the religion of Islam.

**nomad/nomadic** Moving from place to place; without a fixed home.

**Northern Hemisphere** The half of the earth that is above (north of) the equator.

**patriotic/patriotism** Pride and love of country. Waving or saluting your country's flag shows patriotism.

**place** Tells you what a place is like; one of the five ideas that show how geography connects the world.

**plain** A flat, rolling lowland.

**plateau** A large area of flat land that is raised high above the surrounding land.

**porcelain** A hard, white, shiny pottery; china.

**port** Harbor. Ships pull into port to load or unload cargo.

**poverty** Poor; terrible lack. People without food or shelter live in poverty.

**prejudice** An unfair judgment or treatment toward a person or group without cause or reason, often based on someone's race, religion, or ethnic background.

**prophet** A religious teacher; someone who has special spiritual understanding.

**region** Tells you what makes one area like another area; one of the five ideas that show how geography connects the world.

**rural** Country-like; opposite of urban. Much of America's Midwest is rural farmland.

**sacred** Holy places or things.

**scarce** Not much of a supply. In the desert, water is scarce.

**shrine** Structure or place to worship a spirit or being.

**slum** A heavily populated living area that is dirty and run-down.

**Southern Hemisphere** The half of the earth that is below (south of) the equator.

**steeple** A tall, narrow tower on top of a building. Often seen at the top of a church.

**steppe** A flat, treeless plain.

**subcontinent** A large area of land that is a major part of a continent but is a separate geographical or political area. India is a subcontinent of Asia.

**suburb** Areas around the edge of a city or town where people live.

**symbol** Something that stands for something else. Big Ben is a symbol of London, England, throughout the world.

**synagogue** A Jewish building for worship.

**Taoism** An ancient Chinese religion based on the teachings of Lao Zi.

**traditions** Customs; practices or styles that have been used by people for a long time.

**transportation** Way of getting around.

**tsunami** A huge ocean wave caused by an earthquake.

**tundra** A flat, treeless, snow-covered plain. Cold, Arctic-like places like Siberia are usually mostly tundra.

**urban** Heavily populated; city-like.

**veld** South African grassland.

# For More Information

## Further Reading

Banting, Erinn. *Puerto Rico: The People and Culture.* New York: Crabtree Publishing, 2003.

Banting, Erinn. *Puerto Rico: The Land.* New York: Crabtree Publishing, 2003.

Bator, Robert. *Daily Life in Ancient and Modern Istanbul.* Minneapolis, MN: Lerner Publishing, 2000.

Blashfield, Jean F. *England: Enchantment of the World (Second Series).* New York: Children's Press, 2006.

Blauer, Ettagale, and Jason Lauré. *South Africa: Enchantment of the World (Second Series).* New York: Children's Press, 2006.

Burgan, Michael. *From Sea to Shining Sea: Puerto Rico.* New York: Children's Press, 2003.

Dramer, Kim. *People's Republic of China: Enchantment of the World (Second Series).* New York: Children's Press, 2006.

Gordon, Sharon. *Discovering Cultures: Great Britain.* New York: Benchmark Books, 2004.

Heinrichs, Ann. *Brazil: Enchantment of the*

*World (Second Series)*. New York: Children's Press, 2008.

Hintz, Martin. *Israel: Enchantment of the World (Second Series)*. New York: Children's Press, 2006.

Kent, Deborah. *Moscow*. Danbury, CT: Children's Press, 2000.

Murphy, Patricia J. *Discovering Cultures: India*. New York: Benchmark Books, 2003.

Orr, Tamra. *Turkey: Enchantment of the World (Second Series)*. New York: Children's Press, 2003.

Reiser, Robert. *Discovering Cultures: Brazil*. New York: Benchmark Books, 2003.

Rogers, Stillman D. *Russia: Enchantment of the World (Second Series)*. New York: Children's Press, 2002.

Spengler, Kremena. *Israel: A Question and Answer Book*. Mankato, MN: Capstone Press, 2005.

Spengler, Kremena. *South Africa: A Question and Answer Book*. Mankato, MN: Capstone Press, 2006.

Swan, Erin Pembrey. *India: Enchantment of the World (Second Series)*. New York: Children's Press, 2002.

Waryncia, Lou, and Ken Sheldon, editor. *If I Were a Kid in Ancient China*. Peterborough, NH: Cricket Books, 2006.

## Multimedia

*Destination China*. DVD. Globe Trekker, 2005.

*Discovery Atlas: Brazil Revealed*. DVD. The Discovery Channel, 2007.

*Global Treasures: Taj Mahal, India*. DVD. Global Television/Arcadia Films, 2007.

*Israel Today*. DVD. Worldwide Travel Films, 2007.

*Nature Parks: Cape Peninsula. Cape of Good Hope, South Africa*. DVD. Global Television/Arcadia Films, 2007.

*Puerto Rico*. CD-ROM. Puerto Rico Tourism Company, 2005.

*Rails Across Russia: St. Petersburg to the Pacific*. DVD. Globe Scope Productions, 2006.

*Smart Travels Europe: London*. DVD. Smart World Productions, 2003.

*Super Cities: Istanbul*. DVD. International Video Network, 2003.

## Internet Tourism Sites

**Brazil** http://www.braziltourism.org

**China** http://www.cnto.org

**England** http://www.enjoyengland.com

**India** http://www.tourisminindia.com

**Israel** http://www.goisrael.com

**Puerto Rico** http://welcome.topuertorico.org

**Russia** http://www.russia-travel.com

**Turkey** http://www.tourismturkey.org

**South Africa** http://www.southafrica.net

## Embassy Addresses, Telephone Numbers, and Web Sites

**Brazil**

3006 Massachusetts Avenue, NW
Washington, DC 20008
202-238-2700
http://www.brasilemb.org

**England (British Embassy for United Kingdom)**

3100 Massachusetts Avenue, NW

Washington, DC 20008

202-588-7800

http://www.britain-info.org

**China**

2300 Connecticut Avenue, NW

Washington, DC 20008

202-328-2500

http://www.china-embassy.org

**India**

2107 Massachusetts Avenue, NW

Washington, DC 20008

202-939-7000

http://www.indianembassy.org

**Israel**

3514 International Drive, NW

Washington, DC 20008

202-364-5500

http://www.israelemb.org

**Puerto Rico**

La Princesa Building

#2 Paseo la Princesa

Old San Juan, PR 00902

800-866-7827

http://welcome.topuertorico.org

**Russia**

2650 Wisconsin Avenue, NW

Washington, DC 20007

202-298-5700

http://www.russianembassy.org

**Turkey**

2525 Massachusetts Avenue, NW

Washington, DC 20008

202-612-6700

www.turkishembassy.org

**South Africa**

3015 Massachusetts Avenue, NW

Washington, DC 20008

202-232-4400

http://www.saembassy.org

# Index

# Photo Credits